LOW-CARB
Cooking With
STEVIA
The Naturally Sweet & Calorie-Free Herb

James Kirkland

Crystal Health Publishing
Arlington, Texas

Published by:

 Crystal Health Publishing
PO Box 171683
Arlington, TX 76003-1683
United States

Disclaimer:

This book is written for informational purposes only. It is not intended to diagnose or prescribe for any medical condition nor to replace common sense and reasonable caution in consuming stevia products. James Kirkland is not, and does not claim to be, a medical professional, and the information in this book comes from his own experiences and research. If you have any health concerns such as diabetes, cancer, or pregnancy, consult your physician before beginning any new diet or exercise regime. This book should not be used as a substitute for your physicians advice. Neither the authors nor the publisher is responsible for defects in the manufacturing, processing or handling of stevia products. Although the authors and publisher have exhaustively researched all sources to ensure the accuracy of the information contained in this book, we assume no responsibility for errors, inaccuracies, omissions or any other inconsistency herein.

Frequently Asked Stevia Questions, All Stevias Are Not Equal, and Successful Cooking With Stevia from Sugar-Free Cooking With Stevia, 3rd Edition, by James & Tanya Kirkland, copyright © 2000.

Library of Congress Catalog Card Number: 99-98116
Library of Congress Cataloging-in-Publication Data
(Provided by Quality Books, Inc.)
Kirkland, James, 1965-
Low-carb cooking with stevia: the naturally sweet & calorie free herb /
James Kirkland. 1st ed.
p. cm.
    Includes bibliographical references and index.
    ISBN 1-928906-14-1
1. Cookery (Stevia)
2. Stevia Rebaudiana.
3. Low-carbohydrate diet   Recipes. I. Title.
TX 819.S757 2000   641.5635   QB199-1889

*Dedicated to my wife Tanya,
my love, my muse*

Table of Contents

Part One: The Low-Carb Lifestyle

Part Two: Stevia - How Sweet It Is

Part Three: Low-Carb Recipes

Appendix

1

Trials and Triumphs in Health and Cooking

This book is the product of years of frustration with numerous diets and what they did NOT do for me. Like more than 30 percent of Americans, I was overweight, and no matter what I did, I couldn't get those pounds off. I topped the scales at 220 pounds and my cholesterol level was at least that high. I tried everything to lose weight. I ate low-fat this, low-fat that, and as the amount of fat in my diet dropped, my hunger increased to the point where all I thought about was food. Besides that, whatever weight I did lose bounced right back as soon as I stopped following whatever diet I was on. For the longest time I berated myself for my lack of willpower, not realizing my body was trying to tell me something.

In desperation I started exploring other nutritional approaches and stumbled upon 'The New Diet Revolution' by Dr. Atkins and 'Protein Power' by Dr. M.R. Eades and Dr. M.D. Eades. I couldn't believe what I read. For the first time someone was telling me it was okay to eat all the meat I wanted and not worry about the fat. I dove into the Atkins diet and lost 7 pounds in one week. I felt great. I had lots of energy and seldom felt hungry. The menu seemed limited, though, and I started to wonder whether or not this was really for me. I still craved sweets now and again, and wondered if I'd ever be able to eat bread and pasta again.

Around this same time, my wife and I finished our book 'Sugar-Free Cooking with Stevia', which we wrote to help people kick the sugar habit without the use of artificial sweeteners. I used a few of the recipes to add some variety to my new low-carb lifestyle, and this planted the germ of an idea. I looked in the bookstores to see what other low-carb cookbooks were available, and discovered only one among the hundreds of cookbooks on the shelves. Considering the growing profile of the low-carb diets, I thought other people might also feel frustrated by the lack of variety, and decided to combine my knowledge of stevia with what I had learned about the low-carb lifestyle into a cookbook the whole family could enjoy.

It wasn't an easy process. The recipes started out extremely simple—plain meats dressed up in simple sauces. I knew, however, that I had to create something more to justify a cookbook, and so the cooking rampage continued.

I never anticipated just how challenging the whole process would be, and for months my failures matched my successes. Finally, though, I hit the jackpot. One night my wife came home to see me sitting at the table munching on a plateful of fettuccine alfredo, with a huge mess of dirty dishes, pans and other kitchen paraphernalia behind me. She shook her head sadly, asking me if I had lost my patience and succumbed to the lure of pasta. I grinned and informed her that what I was eating was not regular high-carb pasta at all, but almost pure protein! This major break-through led to new and exciting low-carb recipes for pancakes, lasagna, deep-fried stuffed pepper and pasta, among many others.

My main goal with this cookbook was to create low-carb recipes the whole family could enjoy. Often, when one person changes his or her eating habits, either the whole family is forced to change as well, or the person making the change gets little or no support and soon abandons the idea. Including as many 'ordinary' recipes as possible ensures no one will feel coerced or left out. I often serve my low-carb 'potato salad' to guests who never notice the difference from the regular high-carb version.

What you have in your hands is the result of 12 months of my terrorizing the kitchen, using the strangest ingredients in my pursuit of tasty meals. Now, with the help of these recipes, people pursuing the low-carb lifestyle won't have to slog through the monotonous and relentless cycle of eggs, meat, and salad. When I began to miss my old treats in my new low-carb lifestyle, I thought other people would too, and now I'm happy to share what I discovered with other low-carb enthusiasts. The wonderful thing is that these recipes allow you to eat 'normally' without compromising your new and healthy lifestyle.

Since I started following the low-carb dietary guidelines, I've steadily and comfortably lost the excess weight, and my energy level has never been better. My kids love it — now daddy gets in on the games instead of watching from the lawn chair, and they love the new recipes too.

I hope you enjoy them as much as we do.

②

Why the Low-Carb Lifestyle WORKS

For a while I doubted the value of some of the low-carb diets; they seemed too extreme and rigid. However, after thinking about it, the message I took from the low-carb advocates was this: Americans have extremely poor eating habits and these habits are making us fat and unhealthy.

In the 1960's, about 25 percent of Americans were overweight. In 1991, 34 percent of Americans were overweight, and this is after fifteen years of public education on the dangers of saturated fat, which is where we thought the problem lay. Americans eat less saturated fat now than before, yet we're fatter than before! So what's happening here?

One idea put forward by nutritionists and researchers is that the amount of refined sugar we consume has contributed significantly to many health problems, including obesity. Sugar, or sucrose, is a simple carbohydrate and is easily converted into glucose, which is the body's basic fuel. Soft drinks, snack foods, fast foods and pre-packaged foods often contain huge amounts of hidden sugar. The biggest problem with sugar is how the body reacts to it.

When we take in food, stomach acid dissolves it into digestible molecules. Fat and protein take several hours to break down, providing a steadier energy level over a longer period of time. Carbohydrates, especially simple ones like sugar, take almost no time at all to digest, providing instant energy that fades quickly. Sucrose, or refined sugar, is converted into glucose and goes into the bloodstream almost immediately. Blood sugar rises and triggers an insulin response. Insulin, generated by the pancreas, pulls the excess sugar out of the blood and stores it as glycogen for future use, either in the muscles or the liver. Glycogen, not body fat, is the first source of stored energy the body turns to when it needs fuel. If the liver and muscle glycogen stores are full, excess dietary sugar is converted immediately to body fat.

Since the liver and muscles don't have a lot of storage space, about 70 to 80 grams or 273 to 312 calories worth, we don't have to take in many calories in sugar before the body starts storing it as fat. Athletes, of course, burn off the excess quickly and have to eat more to top up their glycogen stores, but sedentary people aren't active enough to use up all their glycogen. If an inactive person's diet is high in carbohydrates, he or she may never start to burn fat, since the body is constantly supplied with all the glucose it needs.

Pasta, bread, whole grains, and starchy vegetables like corn, potatoes, yams and squash are also converted to glucose quickly. Other vegetables are absorbed more slowly, mostly due to their fiber content. Even fruits, which are high in fructose or fruit sugar, affect blood sugar levels less severely than pasta, due to their fiber. To illustrate this, researchers found that the old health-food staple, the rice cake, affects blood sugar levels more drastically than an apple. Interestingly, the food pyramid guide recommends the highest percentage of our food intake be from whole grains and breads. What no one seems to remember, however, is that this guide was originally developed by the agricultural and dairy industries not disinterested medical researchers. The government adapted it as the accepted standard and we've been living with it for more than 30 years, and it is in these past 30 years that our average weight has steadily increased.

To be fair, it's likely that our sugar and junk food habits have more to do with our weight gain than too much rice or oatmeal. To give you an idea of how much sugar we consume, consider these figures. A hundred years ago, Americans consumed 40 pounds of sugar per person per year. As of 1998, Americans consume 148 pounds of sugar per person per year, including children. This equates to almost 4 ounces, or a half a cup, of sugar per day. This may seem hard to believe, but consider that a 16-ounce can of pop contains 1.8 ounces of sucrose/glucose. This means it only takes just over two cans, at 200 calories each, to put a half a cup of sugar in your diet. That doesn't include the donut, the sugar in your coffee or tea, or dessert. For comparison, a large apple contains .5 ounces of fructose (fruit sugar).

Aggressive marketing and product placement by soft-drink companies, snack food producers and fast-food restaurants has made it very easy for

Why the Low-Carb Lifestyle WORKS

us to overindulge. Pop and snack machines in schools, fast food drive-through windows on the way to work, take-out food and pre-packaged dinners offer quick, tasty and convenient solutions to a time-starved population. This food is usually high in saturated fat and carbs, both sugar and starch. These foods make it so easy to eat poorly. It takes time, effort and planning to eat well.

Unfortunately, besides providing unnecessary carbs, these 'convenient' foods also lack the nutrient value of fresh food. Over time, our bodies become starved for vitamins and minerals. We get sick more often, feel tired all the time, and may start to crave more food in an effort to make up for the deficiency. Junk food may contain some nutrients, but it takes a much larger quantity, and many more calories, to get what the body needs. Of course, those extra calories get stored as fat, and the cycle escalates.

Switching from a high-carb diet to a low-carb diet almost automatically eliminates snack foods, pop and fast food. Even huge, meaty hamburgers might have too many carbs for most low-carb dietary guidelines—it's all hidden in the bun, mustard, ketchup, and relish. Eating lean cuts of meat, non-starchy vegetables and some fruit cuts most excess carbs out of the diet without having to monitor anything. Besides that, the vitamin and mineral intake increases dramatically, so the body gets what it needs to function properly.

Fat is GOOD For You

Some people, looking at low-carb diet guidelines, think 'oh my gosh, what about the fat'? We've been told for so long that fat is bad for us, but what most people don't realize, and what most diet books don't tell us, is that the body needs fat to function. Our brain is made up of protein, fatty acids and water. Proper hormone function relies heavily on fatty acids. Every system in our body needs fatty acids at some point.

It isn't so much the amount of fat we consume that matters as much as the type of fat. Animal fat provides a lot of important fatty acids, but in excess it can also contribute to heart disease due to its high level of saturated fat and cholesterol. That's why a healthy low-carb diet relies on lean cuts of meat. Mono- and poly-unsaturated oils are the best source of healthy dietary fats, and are found in nuts and seeds like almonds, walnuts, pumpkin, sunflower seeds and ground flax. Other good plant sources of healthy fats include unrefined, uncooked, olive, sunflower, evening primrose, borage and safflower oils, and good animal sources include cold-water fatty fish like salmon, cod and sole. These foods also provide lots of important trace nutrients and fat-soluble vitamins. Fats provide long-term energy, keep you from feeling hungry, and slow down the digestion of carbohydrates, stopping them from entering the bloodstream too quickly.

We Aren't Designed to Eat Grain

Many proponents of low-carb diets argue that humans are not designed to eat grain. Grain is hard to digest, and in its raw form contains phytates that bind to other nutrients and actually prevent our body from absorbing them. They can also leach essential nutrients from our system if not cooked properly. Original forms of wheat, oats, rye, rice and barley had small kernels and were extremely time-consuming to harvest. When we were in the hunter-gatherer stage, it wasn't worth our time to pick them— we were too busy hunting the animals that grazed on the grain, who digested the stuff much more efficiently. It was only when humans settled down to agriculture ten thousand years ago that we started to utilize grains as a regular food source.

Now ten thousand years may seem like a long time, certainly long enough for people to adapt to a change in diet. Evolution, however, tends to work over hundreds of thousands, even millions, of years. Ten thousand years has not allowed us much time to adapt, and archeologists and paleontologists all seem to agree that the human body has not changed significantly in the last half a million years. So what did people eat before they settled down on the farm? The traditional diet of the few remaining hunter-gatherer tribes gives us an idea: vegetables, roots, fruits, berries, nuts, meat and insects.

Now very few Americans are going to race out and stock up on nightcrawlers for snacks, but what this tells us is that our ancestors ate very few grains, which are actually different kinds of grass seeds. Celiac disease also offers some evidence that not everybody's digestive system has adapted to this relatively modern dietary change. People with celiac disease cannot digest the gluten proteins found in wheat, oats, rye, barley, kamut, spelt or triticale. Demographics show us that people of northern European descent have the highest rate of celiac disease – they were also one of the last groups to settle down into agriculture. Regions with the lowest incidence of celiac disease, like the Middle East and Africa, are also countries that have the longest history of agriculture. So, while some people can handle grains, other groups of people have not had time to adjust, and grains are not necessarily essential to everyone's health.

So What Does Stevia Have to Do With All This?

Whole leaf stevia is 15 times sweeter than sugar, and pure stevioside, the molecule that makes it sweet, is as much as 300 times sweeter than sugar (for more information see chapter 4, All Stevias Are NOT Equal). Stevia has no calories, and does not adversely affect blood sugar levels in its pure form. The aboriginal peoples of Paraguay and Brazil used this native South-American plant for more than 1500 years in drinks and cooking. Japanese researchers have been testing the safety of this herb since the 1970s and have observed no adverse effects, and stevia has been used safely by people with blood sugar, blood pressure and weight problems. Producers of stevia products developed several different forms for consumers, including a liquid extract, syrups and powder. Unlike many artificial sweeteners, stevia does not break down in heat, so it can be used in cooking and baking.

In the United States, Stevia cannot be sold labeled as a 'sweetener'. FDA rulings prohibit labeling it as such, and only allow it to be sold as a dietary supplement or in body care products. I believe pressure from producers of other artificial sweeteners has prevented access to, and knowledge of, this wonderful herb. I could see why they would be leery of a product that holds over 41% of the commercial market in Japan and other Asian countries with a proven excellent health safety record, unlike many of the chemical sweeteners in the US market today. If the FDA authorized labeling stevia as a sweetener, it might very well put companies like Nutrasweet® out of business, or at least cut drastically into their profits. For more information on this issue, please visit my webpage www.CookingWithStevia.com

What stevia means to people following the low-carb lifestyle is that they don't have to give up all their favorite treats. Stevia can be used to replace the sugar in many recipes, with a non-carb filler to make up for the bulk of the sugar replaced. It also means you can sweeten your coffee and tea without counting carbs — it takes only a few drops of liquid stevia extract per one cup of liquid. Many health food stores carry stevia in various forms, so don't hesitate to experiment. In many cases, stevia provided the 'missing link' in making the recipes in this book not only palatable, but delicious.

If you want more recipes using stevia, we also offer the "Sugar-free Cooking with Stevia" cookbook. For more information, contact us at the following address:

Crystal Health Publishing
P.O. Box 171683
Arlington, TX 76003-1683

www.CookingWithStevia.com

3

Frequently Asked Questions

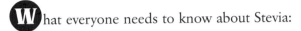hat everyone needs to know about Stevia:

1. What is stevia?

2. Is stevia safe?

3. What are the benefits of using stevia?

4. I have Candidiasis; will using stevia help this problem?

5. Is stevia safe to use during pregnancy or when nursing?

6. I've heard that the natives of South America used stevia as a contraceptive. Does stevia reduce fertility?

7. Does stevia have any effect on hypoglycemia or diabetes?

8. Can stevia stop my sugar cravings?

9. Where is stevia grown?

10. What are the types or forms of stevia?

11. Does stevia perform like sugar when used in cooking and baking? Can I substitute stevia for sugar cup for cup?

12. Will stevia lose its sweetness or break down at high temperatures like aspartame?

13. If stevia has been around so long, why am I just now hearing about it?

14. Why are stevia products so expensive?

15. Why aren't diet soft drinks sweetened with stevia?

16. What are the negative effects of aspartame?

17. What should I look for when purchasing Stevioside or stevia blends?

18. What is Maltodextrin?

19. What is F.O.S.?

1. What is stevia?

Stevia (pronounced steh-via) is a leafy green plant of the Asteraceae family, genus Stevia, species Rebaudiana. Stevia is related to lettuce, marigold and chicory. You may be familiar with stevia by one of its many other names: Sweet Leaf, Caa-he-é, or Erva Doce. Dr. Moises Santiago Bertoni identified and classified this plant in the late 1800's. He named the plant Stevia Rebaudiani Bertoni in honor of a Paraguayan chemist named Rebaudi. The Guarani Indians in South America had been using the leaves of the plant for centuries to sweeten bitter teas and as a sweet treat. When Dr. Bertoni received samples of the plant, he wrote "one small piece of the leaf will keep the mouth sweet for an hour."

2. Is stevia safe?

Is stevia safe? Absolutely. People have used stevia since pre-Columbian times with no reports of ill effects. Decades of research have proven stevia safe for human and animal consumption, unlike some commercial sweeteners

3. What are the benefits of using stevia?

While the following have not been approved or confirmed by the FDA, studies have shown stevia offers the following benefits:

- Sugarless & adds no calories
- 100% natural, not chemically manufactured
- Potent — 250 to 300 times sweeter than table sugar
- Stable to 392 degrees Fahrenheit (200 degrees Celsius)
- Non-fermentable
- Plaque retardant, anti-caries (prevents cavities)
- Does not impact blood sugar levels
- Non-toxic
- Excellent health safety record

4. I have Candidiasis; will using stevia help this problem?

Candidiasis is a fungal yeast overgrowth in the body that thrives on sugar. Remove sugar and you remove its food source. Stevia will not promote fungal growth as it is a sugar-free natural sweetener.

5. Is stevia safe to use during pregnancy or when nursing?

When pregnant or nursing, notify your health professional before taking any dietary supplement or drug.

According to recent research and decades of documented stevioside use in Japan, stevioside has no reported negative side effects when used during pregnancy or nursing. In fact, my wife used stevia during all of her pregnancies and while nursing, and our children have been enjoying stevia tea since infancy. They are all bright, healthy and loved.

6. I've heard that the natives of South America used stevia as a contraceptive. Does stevia reduce fertility?

No, stevia does not reduce fertility. There have been reports of native Paraguayan Indians using the whole green stevia leaves for contraceptive purposes. However, according to modern research, steviosides taken orally do not affect fertility.

7. Does stevia have any effect on hypoglycemia or diabetes?

According to scientific research, stevia does not impact blood sugar levels. It allows the body to regulate blood sugar levels naturally. Of course, if you supplement your stevia-sweetened tea with a Twinkie, all bets are off. Fortunately, if you take care with your diet, stevia is a wonderful way to satisfy cravings for sweets without adding sugars. If you suffer from any type of blood sugar condition, always consult with your physician before using any new product.

8. Can stevia stop my sugar cravings?

Many people report that using stevia has helped them reduce or completely eliminate their sugar cravings. These cravings often occur when the blood sugar becomes low. Sugar gives a quick boost of energy that can feel like a brief 'high', followed by a deep crash as the insulin in the pancreas reacts to store the excess sugar in the liver and muscles, thereby lowering blood sugar levels. Eating a balanced diet with enough protein and fat can help eliminate the energy fluctuations that can lead to sugar cravings. Since stevia does not affect blood sugar levels like sugar, it can help break the sugar cycle.

9. Where is stevia grown?

Originally, stevia grew wild in the regions of Northern Paraguay and Southern Brazil. Today, stevia is grown and used around the world. China, Japan, and other Asian countries, South America, Europe, India, the Ukraine and even North America, grow or import stevia and stevia products.

10. What are the types or forms of stevia? (Also, see chapter 4, All Stevias Are NOT Equal)

STEVIA LEAVES

Fresh Leaves – These have a mild licorice flavor.

Dried Leaves – Dried form of the fresh leaves. Usually about 10-15 times sweeter than sugar. Used in brewing herbal teas and for making liquid extracts.

Tea Cut Leaves – Small pieces that are sifted to remove twigs and other unwanted matter.

Ground Leaves (Powder) – Dried leaves ground into a fine powder. This is used in teas and cooking but does not dissolve.

LIQUID EXTRACTS

Dark – A concentrated syrup made from the dried leaves in a base of water and alcohol. Sweetness may vary between manufacturers. This form offers the greatest amount of benefits from the stevia plant.

Clear – A solution of powdered steviosides dissolved in water, alcohol or glycerin. Sweetness varies between manufacturers.

STEVIOSIDE POWDERED EXTRACTS

'Stevioside' or 'white-powdered stevia' is the purified or processed form of stevia. Removing unwanted plant matter concentrates the sweet glycosides into an off-white powder 200 to 300 times sweeter than sugar. The quality of the powder depends on the purity of the glycosides (i.e. 80-100% pure). The higher the concentration of stevioside, the better the taste.

STEVIA BLENDS

Due to the great strength of the Stevioside Powdered Extracts, manufactures often add filler to "tone" down the strength. This makes the Stevioside easier to use and more palatable. These fillers are usually non-sweet food additives with little to no nutritive value, such as lactose (derived from milk) or maltodextrin. These fillers make the stevia product easier to measure and use in recipes. For more information on stevia blend fillers, see Chapter 4.

11. Does stevia perform like sugar when used in cooking and baking? Can I substitute stevia for sugar cup for cup?

No. The molecular structures of sucrose (sugar) and stevioside differ too much to substitute directly. Sucrose, when heated, will brown or caramelize, making possible such delights as gooey cookies, fudge and caramel. Stevia will not caramelize. In addition, you can not substitute stevia for sugar cup to cup. Because of these differences, cooking with stevia takes some practice. (See Successfully Cooking With Stevia.)

12. Will stevia lose its sweetness or break down at high temperatures like aspartame?

No. One of stevia's biggest advantages is its heat stability. Stevia remains stable to about 392 degrees Fahrenheit, or 200 degrees Celsius, so it can be used in most recipes.

13. If stevia has been around so long, why am I just now learning about it?

Stevia has been around for a long time, even in the United States. Early studies on stevia go back to the 1950's, when the sugar industry fought to prevent the use of stevia in the United States. Greed, corruption and good old-fashioned politics also stood in the way of the public learning about stevia. Today, the manufacturers of chemical sweeteners have lobbied the FDA to prevent stevia's approval as a food additive, even though it has a better health record than any of the chemical sweeteners. If you would like more information, contact "60 Minutes" at CBS. In the Spring of 1997, they aired a report on how the manufacturers of aspartame bought influence with the FDA to push the approval of a sweetener that is now blamed for many illnesses and deaths in America.

14. Why are stevia products so expensive?

Several different factors influence the price of stevia products. As a plant, stevia requires cultivation before it can be harvested for use as a sweetener. This requires large investments of capital to buy plants, farms, equipment, and labor to grow and harvest the plants. Then, there is the expense of processing the leaves into pure stevioside. When compared to sugar and the artificial sweeteners, yes, stevia is expensive; it is not as well-established as the sugar cane industry or as easily produced as the chemical sweeteners. Chemical sweeteners are a blend of inexpensive chemicals that costs very little to manufacture, which is why these companies are so profitable. With more countries growing and processing stevia, prices should soon fall. Also, the newness of stevia to worldwide markets created inefficiencies in delivery and inflated expenses in the supply chain. These should even out as markets become more predictable.

15. Why aren't diet soft drinks sweetened with stevia?

Money, pure and simple. The diet soft drink market is huge, worth billions of dollars, and the manufacturer of aspartame does not want to share that market. Armies of special interest lobbyists were called in to make certain the FDA did not approve stevia for use as a food ingredient. A patent on the aspartame molecule guarantees big profits; stevia is just a natural plant that can be grown by anyone and everyone, and therefore cannot be monopolized.

16. What are the negative effects of aspartame?

Many people chose artificial sweeteners, like aspartame, to replace the sugar in their diet, however, artificial sweeteners have a questionable health record. Aspartame is the number one registered complaint with the FDA, yet it remains approved as a food additive. Aspartame has been linked to several negative effects, including depression of intelligence, loss of short-term memory, gastrointestinal disorders, headaches, visions problems, and seizures.

Ralph G. Walton, MD and Chairman of The Center for Behavioral Medicine and Professor of Clinical Psychiatry, Northeastern Ohio University's College of Medicine, analyzed 164 studies on the health effects of aspartame. Of those 164 cases, 74 had aspartame-related sponsorship and 90 were not funded by the aspartame industry. Of the 90 non-aspartame sponsored studies, 83 (92%) found at least one significant problem with aspartame. Of the 7 studies that found no problems, 6 were conducted by the FDA. Interestingly, several FDA officials involved went to work in the aspartame industry after aspartame was approved as a sweetener.

17. What should I look for when purchasing Stevioside or stevia blends?

For best quality, when purchasing a product with pure steviosides, insist on:

1. A high percentage of steviosides, at least 90%
2. A high percentage of rebaudiosides, at least 20%
3. Unbleached, naturally processed stevioside
4. Organically grown stevia
5. Always buy from a reputable company

18. What is Maltodextrin?

Maltodextrin is a non-sweet complex carbohydrate used as filler in stevia blends, and is virtually tasteless. Maltodextrin can be derived from corn, rice, tapioca, or other starches.

19. What is F.O.S.?

F.O.S. is the common term for fructo-oligosaccharides, which is often blended with Stevioside extract to make 'spoonable stevia'. F.O.S. is a naturally occurring sugar that promotes the growth of certain beneficial internal bacteria. Some people do not tolerate F.O.S. well. These people may experience gas, bloating, or nausea from the use of F.O.S.

4

All Stevias are
NOT Equal

The Many Different Forms of Stevia

Stevia is sold and used in so many different forms that consumers are sometimes bewildered by the choices. This chapter should clear up any confusion about the various forms and uses of stevia, how stevia products are made, and how to choose quality products.

Stevia products generally fall into one of two categories: leaf form or extract. Both have their uses, but it's important to understand what each form can and cannot do.

Leaf Forms

Fresh Leaves

A fresh leaf picked or cut from a stevia plant is the simplest form of the herb. These leaves can be used to make a sweetening extract for sauces and other similar foods, however, the fresh leaves have limited uses. Since the leaves do not dissolve like other sweeteners, they do not work as well in more common sweets like cupcakes or pudding. Please visit our web page at www.CookingWithStevia.com for more information on the simple processes of growing your own stevia plants and making extracts.

Fresh stevia leaves work best in herbal teas. Try steeping a few leaves of stevia with mint, chamomile, or any favorite herb or herbal blend, and you will have a wonderfully sweet, flavorful tea without processed sugar or chemical additives. Before you start using the leaves in your favorite tea, however, steep a few stevia leaves in a cup of hot water and drink the plain fresh stevia tea. This will give you an idea of the potency of stevia's sweetness and let you taste stevia's own unique flavor. Yes, stevia has its own taste — most people describe the natural taste as a mild licorice flavor. Refined sugar, in contrast, is so processed that its natural flavor has been lost. Chemical sweeteners, designed to imitate the taste, or lack thereof, of table sugar, still exhibit a faint chemical aftertaste. Natural sweeteners you might have in your kitchen include corn syrup, molasses, pure maple syrup or honey, and like stevia, each provides sweetness and has its own distinct taste. Their one disadvantage is that they all add calories and sugars. Stevia allows you to sweeten food and beverages without adding calories, sugars or artificial chemicals to your diet.

Dried Stevia Leaves

These are simply fresh stevia leaves that are dried to remove all water, allowing for an extended storage period. The easiest way to dry stevia leaves is with a dehydrator, following the manufacturers instructions for drying herbs. Drying them in an oven on the lowest setting will work as well, but check them often, and don't leave them in longer than a few hours. Traditionally, the stevia leaves were harvested on a farm and allowed to dry under the hot South American summer sun. Dried stevia leaves have basically the same uses as fresh leaves.

Ground Stevia Leaves (Green Powdered Stevia)

Like most other herbs, stevia can be ground up. While we add ground oregano for its particular flavor, we only want stevia's sweetness. When stevia was first ground up, the intention was to use the ground leaves like sugar. However, sugar dissolves in liquids, ground stevia leaves do not. Finely ground stevia leaves can be used in the same manner as fresh or dried stevia leaves, but they still fall short when making a pie or cake. I remember making a vanilla pudding with ground leaves, once. The end result was a pasty green pudding that had more licorice taste than vanilla. Yes, you can cook with the ground leaves but other stevia products will help you get the results you want.

Stevia Dark Liquid Extract

(Stevia Syrup)

The simplest form of stevia extract is a syrup made by re-hydrating dried stevia leaves with water, then cooking down the mixture to make a thick liquid. Stevia syrup sounds good, but it requires a little getting used to. A dark, greenish-black liquid, stevia syrup is 100 to 150 times sweeter than simple sugar syrup, depending on its concentration. This is not like maple syrup or corn syrup. The regular stevia leaf has a slight licorice taste; now imagine that mild flavor a 100 times stronger. The intense licorice taste can be very bitter, so use this extremely concentrated extract sparingly. In an 8 oz. glass of water, 3 to 10 drops, depending on the brand and concentration, is enough. This produces a glass of stevia 'tea', but when mixed with coffee, tea or other beverages, it works well. Will these other drinks have that unique stevia flavor? Probably. It depends on the brand of stevia syrup and how much you use. Some flavors, like lemon, can mask or hide stevia's natural flavor.

Since liquids can spoil, some form of preservative is needed. Some manufacturers use alcohol — often 18% alcohol or higher (that's 36 proof - as much as some liqueurs). Some stevia companies use a more palatable preservative such as grapefruit seed extract, chrysanthemum flower, or some other form of approved preservative. Be sure to read the labels carefully to avoid buying products with an additive you might not want. You can even make your own home grown Stevia Dark Syrup.

Stevia Dark Syrup

Grow it yourself and this is the most economical stevia extract ever!

3 cups of packed, crushed, dried stevia leaves
Approximately 4 cups of water
Everclear alcohol (195 proof)
At least 4 clean 2-oz containers with dropper top, available from the pharmacy
Pantyhose, for straining the syrup.
Store bought Stevia Dark Syrup, for comparative testing

In a crock-pot combine 3½ cups of water and 3 cups of crushed stevia leaves that are firmly packed. The stevia/water mixture should be the consistency of mud and may resemble cooked spinach. If the mixture seems too dry add more water. With the lid on, allow to simmer on lowest heat for 48 hours stirring occasionally. Add more water as needed. After 48 hours, allow the mixture to cool. Spoon the stevia pulp into the foot of clean pantyhose. You may want to cut the pantyhose well above the knee if you are making a large batch. Over the crock-pot, squeeze as much stevia liquid out of the stevia pulp as possible (about 3 cups of liquid). With the lid off, gently boil stevia liquid until it is reduced by ⅔. Syrup should be about the consistency of molasses, dark, and super sweet. It normally yields about ⅓–½ cup of Green Stevia Syrup from this recipe.

*If desired, you may re-seep the stevia pulp 2 or 3 times. However, this will only slightly increase the end product.

Preserving: Allow the syrup to cool. Using a small funnel, pour 1½ tablespoons of syrup in each bottle. Then add ½ tablespoon of Everclear. This will result in approximately 25% alcohol content, or 50 proof. Screw lids on tightly and shake. Store away from direct sun or heat.

Testing for Sweetness: Because some recipes call for green syrup, it is important to be familiar with the different sweetening ability in order to make recipe adjustments. You can dilute the strength of your syrup by adding more alcohol, or increase the sweetening by adjusting the cooking time the next time you make syrup.

In an 8-oz cup of water stir in ¼ teaspoon of Green Stevia Syrup. In a different 8-oz cup of water stir in ¼ teaspoon of Store Bought Syrup. Compare.

Makes approximately 4, 2-oz bottles of Green Stevia Syrup

Stevia Steviosides

(Commonly called White Stevia Powder, or Pure Stevioside Extract)

Steviosides, a group of sweet tasting molecules (glycosides), give the stevia herb its amazing sweetness. With a taste up to 300 times sweeter than sugar, Steviosides have no fat, no calories, no processed sugars and no carbohydrates. Actually, researchers have identified eight sweet glycosides within the leaves of the stevia plant, but the three best tasting are Stevioside, Rebaudioside A and Rebaudioside B. Since Rebaudiosides A, B and five other sweet molecules occur in such small amounts, they are grouped together under the singular term 'stevioside' for convenience.

Pure Stevioside extract can range in color from creamy off-white with a hint of green to stark paper white. Its taste can vary from bitter, licorice, or saccharine-like to that of super-sweet powdered sugar. The Japanese have been using pure stevioside since the 1970s, and this natural extract constitutes more than 41 percent of Japan's commercial sweetener market. Pure Stevioside extract also provides the base for several stevia products, including liquid stevia extract, spoonable stevia/stevia blends, and quick-dissolving stevia tablets.

Stevioside Quality

The quality of any stevia product depends on the actual amount of steviosides it contains, the percentage of rebaudiosides, the cultivation and extraction methods, and whether or not any questionable additives were present at any time during growing, harvesting or processing.

Amount of Steviosides

The quality of the stevioside extract that you purchase is based predominantly on the amount of steviosides it contains. Some 'pure stevioside extracts' contain about 70% steviosides. The other 30% is made up of undesirable plant components. This 30% can give the extract a strong licorice, bitter, or an unpleasant aftertaste. Generally speaking, a stevioside percentage of at least 85% should yield good flavor with minimal bitterness.

Percentage of Rebaudiosides

The other sweet glycosides can also help improve the taste of a stevioside extract. In the world of stevia extracts, Rebaudioside A and B are the gold at the end of the rainbow. These glycosides have incredible sweetness with no bitterness, no licorice taste, and no unpleasant aftertaste. Unfortunately, rebaudiosides make up just a scant 3% of the stevia plant. In Japan, where stevia technology is the most advanced, extracts with a high concentration of rebaudiosides are common. I once received samples of a Japanese stevioside, which was almost entirely rebaudiosides — Wow! It tasted just like 300x sweet powdered sugar. Unfortunately, the Japanese consume as much stevioside extract as they produce, making it impossible to currently purchase this purity in the United States.

As a consumer, you can ask manufacturers what percentage of rebaudiosides their products contain; anything over 20% is good. The highest percentage I've located in the U.S. is 30% rebaudiosides. If the manufacturer doesn't know the percentage, or worse, doesn't know what rebaudiosides are, find another source.

Cultivation

Although stevia grows wild, the most potent hybrids are cultivated on farms throughout the world. Rich in steviosides and rebaudiosides, these plants can vary in stevioside content from 5 to 18%. Several companies also use organic farming techniques for added peace of mind.

Extraction Methods

There exist various methods of processing steviosides and dozens of technical patents describing how to extract steviosides from the plant. The most common methods use alcohol, chemical solvents, gases or water to separate the desirable steviosides from the unwanted plant material. Most often a combination of several methods is used. Water extraction techniques generally create a better tasting product.

After or during the extraction process, some companies decolorize, or bleach, the stevioside. This is an unnecessary step done to give the appearance of white sugar or artificial sweeteners. Natural stevioside should be creamy beige with just a hint of its original green.

Questionable Additives

As a stevia industry consultant, I constantly receive stevioside samples from around the world. Unfortunately, I occasionally receive samples from

China and Korea with artificial sweeteners listed as ingredients, or worse, not listed but included in the product, which I discovered only after having the sample analyzed in a lab. Combining steviosides and artificial sweeteners not only hides the bitter taste of low quality stevioside, but also makes the product cheaper to produce, increasing the profit margin.

In addition to artificial sweeteners, other undesirable residues may also be present. For example, in 1999, the FDA confiscated over 8 shipments of "white" Stevia extract powder coming into the USA from Asia because they were found to be impure. In 1995 only four major companies sold powdered stevioside extract. Today dozens of companies are trying to get onto the stevia bandwagon — especially 'mom & pop' outfits that buy low-grade stevioside then repackage and sell it from their homes. They may knowingly or unknowingly be selling adulterated stevioside. To avoid these rip-offs, purchase stevia only from reputable companies with a history of dealing with the herb. If you aren't sure, ask for a certificate of analysis.

Product Descriptions of Stevioside Based Extracts

Clear Liquid Stevia Extract

When stevia users complained about the bitter, licorice taste of the whole leaf syrup extracts, the suppliers started making liquid extracts or liquid solutions with stevioside. Dissolving the pure stevioside into water creates a product that is sweet, concentrated, attractive and pleasant tasting. This is also extremely profitable to manufacture. You can make your own clear liquid extract for a fraction of the cost (see recipe below).

Clear Liquid Stevia Extract

Both economical and easy!

2-ounce dropper bottle (available in most pharmacies)
¾ teaspoon pure stevioside extract
1½ tablespoons warm water
½ tablespoon Everclear alcohol (as a preservative)
Alternative:
Substitute ½ tablespoon Everclear alcohol for water — must keep refrigerated

In a small dropper bottle, combine 1½ tablespoons warm water with ¾ teaspoons of pure stevioside extract. Cap tightly and shake well. Add ½ tablespoon alcohol or ½ tablespoon water

---

A liquid solution is especially convenient for sweetening beverages and cereals. However, because the sweetness varies so much from manufacture to manufacture, the clear liquid extract is NOT recommended for cooking.

The quality of clear liquid stevia extract depends on two factors:

1. The quality of the stevioside used to make the extract.

2. The type of preservative used, such as alcohol, chrysanthemum flower, or grapefruit seed extract. Check labels to ensure it doesn't contain a preservative you might not want.

Stevia Blends (commonly called 'Spoonable Stevia')

Simply the best! My children love to eat Spoonable Stevia right from the jar!

Stevia blends combine pure stevioside extract with a filler to make an easy-to-measure great tasting powder. These blends are by far the most versatile and easy-to-use form of stevia available.

Using fillers to tone down sweetness isn't a new idea. When consumers first used Saccharin, they complained that it was far too sweet, so the manufacturers blended saccharin with a non-nutritive filler such as maltodextrin to make their sweetener easier for users to measure. Some stevia companies have followed this example, taking a product 300 times sweeter than sugar and creating one only four times sweeter than sugar (a 4:1 stevia blend to sugar ratio). Although not a formal industry standard, it is the most popular ratio.

Stevia blends are so easy to use. Spoon them over cereal, fruit, or add to beverages. Stevia blends will mainstream stevia as a sweetener for the future because of its wonderful flavor and ease of use.

Types of Fillers used in Stevia Blends or 'Spoonable Stevia'

The following fillers add ease-of-use with minimal caloric impact. Currently, the most common fillers used for stevia blends are dextrose, maltodextrin, lactose, and F.O.S.

- Dextrose is a common processing agent derived from corn sugar. It keeps other components from clumping.

- Lactose is derived from milk; it has a slightly sweet taste and dissolves instantly, even in ice water. People with milk intolerance might want to avoid products with lactose as filler.

- Maltodextrin is a non-sweet complex carbohydrate that is virtually tasteless. Maltodextrin can be derived from corn, rice, tapioca, or other starches and has a very low glycemic index.

- F.O.S. is the common term for fructo-oligosaccharides. F.O.S. is a sugar found in a variety of common foods, like bananas, garlic, and wheat. Although mildly sweet tasting, F.O.S. has a very low glycemic index. F.O.S. also promotes the growth of some beneficial internal bacteria such as Acidophilus, Bifidus and Faecium. F.O.S. is not toxic, however, some people do not tolerate F.O.S. well. These people may experience gas, bloating, or nausea from the use of F.O.S.

Stevia Packets

Stevia packets normally contain the same ingredients as stevia blends, except in convenient, pre-measured servings. Although convenient when on the go, they are generally more expensive than stevia blends in bulk form.

Stevia Quick Dissolving Tablets

These tablets are rather new on the market. They normally contain stevioside along with other ingredients, and are mainly used to sweeten beverages. Some, however, may only dissolve in hot liquids.

Quick Tips for Purchasing High Quality Stevioside Products:

For best quality, when purchasing a product with pure steviosides, insist on:

1. A high percentage of steviosides, at least 90%

2. A high percentage of rebaudiosides, at least 20%

3. Unbleached, naturally processed stevioside

4. Organically grown stevia

5. Buying from a reputable company

How to read labels

When you purchase a jar of 'pure stevioside extract' the ingredients will usually read something as follows:

(Brand A) INGREDIENTS: 85% steviosides – stevia rebaudiana bertoni (sweet leaf) *or*

(Brand B) INGREDIENTS: Stevia Rebaudiana Bertoni (96% concentrated steviosides; total amount of rebaudiosides, 30%) *or*

(Brand C) INGREDIENTS: 100% Stevia Rebaudiana Bertoni Extract

By law all stevioside supplements must list stevia by its full scientific name, stevia rebaudiana bertoni. Asides from that, the labels can vary greatly.

Brand A gives its stevioside percentage, then its scientific name followed by a common name of the stevia herb (sweet leaf).

Brand B states the scientific name, then the amount of steviosides and the percentage of rebaudiosides.

However, brand C's claim of being 100% stevia is true, but NOT 100% steviosides. (Brand A and B are also 100% stevia.)

Brand C did not even list its stevioside concentration. Often, if a brand does not list the percentage of steviosides, then you can bet it is low. Labels can be difficult to read. If you have any questions, call the manufacturer.

5

Successful Cooking
With Stevia

How to Enjoy the Low-Carb Lifestyle

Most of us crave sweets, but let's face it, processed sugar doesn't do us any good. It adds empty calories without any beneficial nutrients, and sugar has been linked to a variety of ailments including candidiasis, hyperactivity, and some types of diabetes. Sugar Blues, by William Dufty, is an excellent book about the problems associated with refined sugar.

Step one to kicking the sugar habit is replacing processed sugar with nature's sweetener: stevia. The term 'stevia' in this chapter refers exclusively to stevioside products, such as pure stevioside, stevia blend, or packets (for the different forms of stevia, see Chapter 4). You can substitute stevia in your favorite recipes by following a few simple tips. Since stevia extracts are so highly concentrated, a little goes a long way — you can replace a whole cup of sugar with just a small amount of stevia. Be sure and follow our conversion charts carefully for the best results.

Tips For Cooking With Stevia

The first thing to remember is that stevia is sweet, but not exactly like sugar. Comparing stevia to sugar is like comparing molasses to honey or maple syrup to corn syrup. All are sweet but each one has a unique taste, and, when properly used, can produce wonderful results in many types of recipes.

The next step to using this herb successfully is understanding how its sweetness differs from refined sugars. Add a few drops of a non-alcohol stevia extract to a glass of water. Taste it. Its sweetness will differ from the refined sugars and chemicals sweeteners. Add one drop of clear liquid extract at a time and taste after each one until the mixture becomes bittersweet. It is this bitter-sweetness that can sometimes make stevia difficult to work with — you will soon get the hang of using just the right amount.

Some people love the taste of stevia while others take a while to adjust to the mild licorice taste. One way to make the transition is to add a little natural sugar like honey, pure maple syrup, or even white grape juice concentrate until your taste buds adjust to the natural sweetness of stevia. In just a short while, you should be able to use stevia alone.

Cooking with stevia can have some limitations. Stevia does not brown or caramelize like sugar. Stevia does not add volume and texture, as do conventional sweeteners. Therefore, baked goods, especially cakes, may not rise as well, and achieving that soft chewy cookie texture will take a little practice. Don't despair — in this book, you will find many secrets and great recipes for successful cooking with stevia.

Helpful Hints

COOKIES:

Always preheat the oven to the recommended temperature. Crisp, shortbread types of cookies give the best results. For softer, chewy cookies, add some canned pumpkin, uncooked oatmeal or even peanut butter. Never over-bake soft cookies — keep an eye on them in the oven. Another way to achieve a softer cookie texture is with bar or pan cookies like brownies. Their texture and thickness will help satisfy your chewy cookie cravings.

CAKES:

Always preheat the oven to the recommended temperature. One secret to moist and light cakes is separating the egg whites and whipping them to supper-stiff peaks before folding in the other ingredients, similar to making an angel food cake. After removing the cooked cake from the oven, immediately invert the pan onto a cooling rack. This prevents the cake from falling.

FLAVORINGS AND EXTRACTS:

Flavorings and extracts such as maple, lemon, and vanilla are great ways to mask the natural licorice flavor of stevia, while adding depth and interest to your dish.

DAIRY:

Stevia extracts work great with milk, cream, cream cheese, sour cream and other dairy products. That is why we use dairy products in so many of our recipes.

If you are dairy or lactose-intolerant, try replacing the milk with Almond Milk (see index), soy milk, or rice milk (both soy milk and rice milk are available at health stores). In fact, fresh soy milk contains fewer carbohydrates that whole cow's milk. Vegetable milks work well, but store-bought vegetable milks often have added sugar, so read the labels carefully.

BEVERAGES:

This is the easiest place to use stevia. A few drops of clear liquid extract or a pre-measured packet can replace the sugar in traditionally sugar-laden drinks like iced or hot teas, coffee, lemonade, and pre-mixed drink powders.

BREADS:

Yeast Bread: A common misconception is that yeast breads won't rise without sugar to act as a catalyst. However, bread can rise with just the flour to feed the yeast; this process just takes longer.

Quick Breads: As with cakes, stevia-sweetened quick breads tend not to rise as well as conventionally sweetened breads. We have made adjustments in the amounts of baking powder or soda in our recipes to give you amazingly delicious sugar-free muffins and breads.

Adding the stevioside: The key to good taste

(See chapter 4 for essential information about stevioside)

The final secret to successful cooking with this herb is using a quality stevioside product and carefully blending it with all other ingredients. Stevia blends (see Types of Stevia, Chapter 4) are the easiest to work with. If you use a bit too much, it won't ruin the recipe. However, pure stevioside is so concentrated that you must measure carefully; just a pinch too much and your wonderful creation may only be fit to feed to the garbage can. We recommend thoroughly mixing pure stevioside with the dry ingredients before adding the wet ingredients. or completely dissolving the stevioside in one of the liquid ingredients (stevioside dissolves faster in warm liquids). Cooking with clear liquid stevioside is generally not recommended because its sweetness varies so greatly from manufacture to manufacture. Whatever the type of stevia extract used, thoroughly combine it with all the other ingredients or your baked goods may not turn out as you expect.

Stevia: The First Step Towards the Low-Carb Lifestyle

OBVIOUS CARBS AND HIDDEN CARBS

Sugar: Sugar is an obvious no-no on the low-carb diet — not only is it a carbohydrate nightmare at 200 grams of carbs per cup, refined sugars contain virtually no nutritional value.

The numerous artificial sweeteners, approved by the FDA, offer an alternative, but independent research questions the safety of several of these products. Reports have linked certain artificial sweeteners with cancer, chronic fatigue, Alzheimer's disease, seizures and neurological damage.

Stevia offers the healthiest calorie-free alternative to sugar and artificial sweeteners

Potatoes: Potatoes are vegetables, so we assume they are healthy. While they do supply useful nutrients, they also contain a lot of carbohydrates: 1 cup contains 30 grams. Although not perfect, cooked cauliflower, at 5 grams of carbs per cup, has a similar texture and can be used to thicken soups instead of potatoes or flour.

Corn: Corn on the cob may almost be an American tradition, but with 34 grams of carbs per cup, corn can really help us pack on the pounds.

Rice: 1 cup of cooked rice has 44 grams of carbohydrates. For a great side dish with a similar texture, try shredding zucchini, seasoning, then lightly sauté until hot.

Pasta: 6 ounces of spaghetti contains 126 grams of carbohydrates. Ouch.

Wheat Flour: Enjoying wheat breads, cakes, and cookies are what I missed most in the beginning on my new low-carb life. Fortunately, I discovered I can still enjoy these staples of the American diet in moderation by using high protein substitutes. When used in the right combination, soy flour, gluten, isolated soy and whey protein all offer excellent alternatives to high-carb flour. Although the taste and texture does not exactly mimic wheat flour, it's very close, and after awhile you won't remember the difference.

Low-Carb Baking Mix

The closest thing to low-carb flour

Low-Carb Baking Mix can be used to make most breads, pancakes, used as a coating for fried or breaded foods and to help thicken gravies.

4 cups Isolated Soy Protein	950 ml
2 cup soy flour	475 ml
4 tablespoons baking soda	60 ml
2 teaspoons salt	10 ml
2 teaspoons stevia blend	10 ml

Sift together all ingredients. Store in an airtight container in a cool dry place. Makes about 5 cups or 12 ½-cup servings

Vegetables and Fruits: Fresh fruits and vegetables provide lots of vitamins and minerals, but they vary widely in the number of carbohydrates they contain. Green leafy vegetables and non-citrus fruits like apples and pears contain lower amounts of carbs than sweet root veggies and tropical fruits like bananas, oranges and mangoes.

Protein: Your first sources of protein will be the same proteins most Americans have eaten for decades: chicken, beef, pork, fish, and eggs. You will find you can add more protein to your diet by substituting carbohydrates with the low-carb flour substitute. Getting enough good protein into your diet will not be a problem. Lean proteins work best as they don't contain high levels of saturated fat.

Fats: Although fats are a high calorie component of any diet, they are also vital to good health. Every system in our bodies requires fatty acids to function, and the higher quality the fat you take in, the better everything works. Excess animal fat, while providing essential fatty acids, contributes to heart disease. Mono and poly-unsaturated fats like unrefined olive, sunflower and safflower oils offer healthier choices. Since fat plays an important part in how food tastes, I strongly suggest that you invest in quality. Buy the best tasting extra-virgin olive oil, throw away the margarine, and stock up on real butter. Invest in high quality vegetable oil if you like fried foods. Find an oil that does not break down or 'hydrogenate' at high temperatures, and never reuse oils for cooking or frying. Different oils include peanut, canola, and corn oils, which all have a slightly different taste and aroma. Because olive oil has a very strong flavor, it works best for salad dressings and low-heat cooking.

Snack Foods — What good is the dip without the chips?

Salty Snacks: Granted, potato chips are out of the question in a low-carb lifestyle, but there are some great substitutes. Cheese Crisps are my family's favorite snack. They take just a few minutes to make, and clean up is a snap. Low-carb Tortillas are another great snack, and you can buy them from health food stores or make your own. Of course, celery sticks, the traditional standby, work wonderfully with dips and spreads.

Cheese Crisps

Here's a quick recipe sample

1 cup of shredded cheddar cheese
Various spices (optional)

In a lightly oiled non-stick skillet, sprinkle about 1 cup of shredded cheddar cheese in a thin layer. Allow to cook over medium high heat till melted and bubbly. When the bottom of the cheese becomes firm and slightly brown, flip it over with a spatula and allow the other side to brown slightly. Remove and place on paper towels to absorb excess oil. Using a sharp knife or pizza cutter, cut the cheese while still hot. Allow to cool and enjoy plain or with your favorite low-carb dip.

VARIATIONS

Instead of cheddar, substitute Parmesan, Swiss, Colby, or combinations of various hard cheeses. Spice it up sprinkle Cajun spices, chopped onions, or bacon bits. Let your taste buds go wild.

Nuts & Seeds: These bite-sized wonders are another family favorite, plus they contain unsaturated fats, and many beneficial nutrients. Of course, you don't have to settle for plain, undecorated nuts. Enjoy Almonds, Harvest Pecans, Sweet Maple Pecans, and Stevia Roasted Peanuts. The possibilities are endless.

On-The-Go Energy

Not being able to grab a candy bar when on the go can be a problem. Fortunately, many brands of high protein bars are now available at health food stores. You can even make your own Protein Bar (see index). Low-carb cupcakes or muffins also make for great on-the-go dining. Besides the fact my wife and kids keep me busy, my day job takes me on long business trips where I often find myself driving endless hours with nothing but an occasional gas station to refuel and get a bite to eat. What can I possibly find to eat at a gas station? They all have meat, cheese, nuts, and other snack foods, but many are sweetened with sugar of some kind or another, or are high in starches. So, I plan ahead. I either make my own protein bars or buy pre-made bars like The Zone or Atkins Bars from health food stores. I take along homemade powdered drink mixes like Hot Coco Mix (see index) or buy Stevita Energy Drink Mixes. I also take lots of pre-measured stevia packets to dress up my glass of water (with a touch of lemon) when dining out. Stevia, and planning ahead, has helped me stick to my low-carb lifestyle, so I don't have to suffer the traveler's stomach when working. The low-carb diet has given me energy, stamina and health I thought I would never taste again.

6

Beverages

Beverages

Almond Milk

A cool summer treat

4 cups cold water	1 liter
1 cup almonds	240 ml
¼ teaspoon stevioside	1.25 ml
or 2 teaspoons stevia blend	10 ml
or 4 packets of stevia	

Soak almonds in a bowl with four cups of water overnight. In a blender or food processor, combine soaked almonds, water, and stevia. Puree on high speed for 2 minutes or until smooth. The resulting liquid may be a little bit grainy. If you don't like the texture, filter the milk through a fine screen mesh. Refrigerate unused portion. Keeps about 5 days.

Makes approximately five 1-cup servings.

NUTRITIONAL FACTS PER SERVING: 6G CARBOHYDRATE; 167 CALORIES; 15G TOTAL FAT; 6G PROTEIN • FOOD EXCHANGES: ½ STARCH; ½ LEAN MEAT; 2½ FAT

Spiced Tea

For the holidays

4 cups water	1 liter
4 cinnamon sticks	4
2 teaspoons allspice	10 ml
2 teaspoons cloves	10 ml
4 tea bags	4
4 cups water	1 liter
3¾ teaspoons stevioside	19 ml
or 8½ teaspoons stevia blend	128 ml
or 17 packets of stevia	
1 teaspoon orange extract	5 ml
1 teaspoon lemon extract	5 ml
8 cups water	2 liters

In a large pot, bring 4 cups of water, spices and stevioside to a boil. Add tea bags and allow to steep for 5 minutes. Remove bags and add 4 more cups of water. Bring to a boil and then steep for 15 minutes. Add extracts and remaining water. Adjust water amount to desired taste and strength. Store in large containers and refrigerate. Serve cold.

Makes 16 servings

NUTRITIONAL FACTS PER SERVING: 3G CARBOHYDRATE; 12 CALORIES; TRACE TOTAL FAT; TRACE PROTEIN • FOOD EXCHANGES: FREE

Eggnog

A holiday classic

6 eggs, lightly beaten	6
2 cups whole milk	475 ml
1 cup heavy cream	235 ml
⅜ teaspoon stevioside	1.8 ml
or 3 teaspoons stevia blend	15 ml
or 6 packets of stevia	
1 teaspoon vanilla extract	5 ml

Garnish
4 tablespoons whipped cream	60 ml
½ teaspoon cocoa or cinnamon	2.5 ml

In a large saucepan, mix eggs, milk, cream and stevia. Cook over medium heat, stirring constantly, until mixture coats a metal spoon. Remove from heat. Cool quickly by placing pan in a sink or bowl of ice and continue stirring for a few minutes. Add vanilla. Chill 4 to 24 hours. Top each serving with whipped cream, if desired, and sprinkle with choice of garnish.

Makes 4 servings

NUTRITIONAL FACTS PER SERVING: 9G CARBOHYDRATE; 408 CALORIES; 35G TOTAL FAT; 14G PROTEIN • FOOD EXCHANGES: 1 LEAN MEAT; 6½ FAT

Hot Cocoa

Hot and creamy and the perfect winter warmer

8 ounces heavy cream	235 ml
12 ounces water	355 ml
2 teaspoons cocoa powder	10 ml
¼ teaspoon stevioside	1.25 ml
or 2 teaspoons stevia blend	10 ml
or 4 packets of stevia	
¼ teaspoon vanilla	1.25 ml

In a saucepan, mix cream and water and bring to a simmer of low heat. Stir constantly. When cream mixture gets hot, add cocoa, stevia and vanilla and continue to stir until dissolved. Serve hot.

Makes 2 servings

NUTRITIONAL FACTS PER SERVING: 4G CARBOHYDRATE; 397 CALORIES; 42G TOTAL FAT; 3G PROTEIN • FOOD EXCHANGES: 8½ FAT

Instant Spiced Cocoa Mix

⅓ cup cocoa powder	80 ml
2 cups powdered milk	475 ml
¾ teaspoon stevioside	3.7 ml
or 6 teaspoons stevia blend	30 ml
or 12 packets of stevia	
½ teaspoon cinnamon	2.5 ml
½ teaspoon cloves	2.5 ml
¼ teaspoon nutmeg	1.25 ml
¼ teaspoon ginger	1.25 ml

In a food processor, combine all ingredients until well blended. To make cocoa (hot), add 3 tbsp. of powder mix to a mug of boiling water. For richer cocoa, add ¼ cup of heavy cream for 1 extra carbohydrate.

Yield: twelve 3-tablespoon servings

NUTRITIONAL FACTS PER SERVING: 10G CARBOHYDRATE; 112 CALORIES; 6G TOTAL FAT; 6G PROTEIN • FOOD EXCHANGES: 1 FAT

Note: If you want only an instant cocoa mix, simply omit the spices.

Summer Cappuccino

Cappuccino Semifreddo (see Index)
Almond Milk (see Index)

In small dessert cups, spoon ½ cup of the Cappuccino Semifreddo into each cup. Pour Almond Milk over Cappuccino Semifreddo until about ⅓ of it is covered. Garnish with nutmeg, cocoa powder or a slice of fruit.

Makes ½-cup servings

NUTRITIONAL FACTS PER SERVING: 10G CARBOHYDRATE; 385 CALORIES; 36G TOTAL FAT; 8G PROTEIN • FOOD EXCHANGES: ½ STARCH; ½ LEAN MEAT; 7 FAT

Iced Cappuccino

1 teaspoon orange zest, optional	5 ml
1½ cups coffee, brewed	355 ml
7½ cups cold water	1¾ liters
⅜ teaspoon stevioside	2.5 ml
or 3 teaspoons stevia blend	15 ml
or 6 packets of stevia	
1½ cups whole milk	355 ml
1½ cups heavy cream	355 ml

Garnish:

10 tablespoons whipped cream (see Index)	265 ml
cocoa, nutmeg or cinnamon	

Place orange zest in bottom of coffee pot. Brew coffee using cold water and espresso; cool to room temperature. Strain coffee and discard orange zest; stir in stevia, milk and cream. Refrigerate until well chilled. Pour cappuccino into glasses; spoon small dollops of whipped cream on each and sprinkle with cocoa, nutmeg or cinnamon.

Makes 10 servings

NUTRITIONAL FACTS PER SERVING: 3G CARBOHYDRATE; 172 CALORIES; 17G TOTAL FAT; 2G PROTEIN • FOOD EXCHANGES: 3½ FAT

Kahlúa

10 tablespoons instant coffee	150 ml
1¼ teaspoons stevioside	6.25 ml
or 10 teaspoons stevia blend	50 ml
or 20 packets of stevia	
1 quart water	1 liter
1 quart vodka	1 liter
3 tablespoons vanilla	45 ml

In a large saucepan, combine coffee, stevia and water and simmer until dissolved. Cool in refrigerator until very cold. Add the vodka and vanilla. Stir thoroughly. Pour into a bottle and store.

Makes 2 quarts or 10 servings

NUTRITIONAL FACTS PER SERVING: 2G CARBOHYDRATE; 219 CALORIES; TRACE PROTEIN • FOOD EXCHANGES: 0 EXCHANGES

Family Punch

1 packet Kool-Aid® brand unsweetened mix	1 packet
⅜ teaspoon stevioside	1.85 ml
or 3 teaspoons stevia blend	15 ml
or 6 packets of stevia	
2 quarts cold water	2 liters

Empty packet contents into a large plastic or glass pitcher. Add stevia and water and mix well until powder is dissolved. Serve cold.

Makes eight 1-cup servings.

NUTRITIONAL FACTS PER SERVING: 0 NUTRITION • FOOD EXCHANGES: 0 EXCHANGES

Lemonade Concentrate

2 teaspoons stevioside	10 ml
or 16 teaspoons stevia blend	80 ml
or 32 packets of stevia	
2½ cups water	595 ml
9 whole lemons	9
sprigs of mint	

Combine stevia and water in a small saucepan and mix over medium heat until stevia has dissolved. Reserve one lemon to slice for garnish. Grate zest of 2 lemons; juice 8 lemons. Combine juice and zest with warm syrup. Steep one hour. Strain.

To serve: Mix 1 part lemonade concentrate with 2 parts water. Serve over ice. Garnish with lemon slices and mint.

Makes 24 servings

NUTRITIONAL FACTS PER SERVING: 2G CARBOHYDRATE; 4 CALORIES; TRACE TOTAL FAT; TRACE PROTEIN • FOOD EXCHANGES: 0 EXCHANGES

Classic Lemonade/Limeade

4 cups water	1 liter
1 cup lemon juice	235 ml
¼ teaspoon stevioside	1.25 ml
or 2 teaspoons stevia blend	10 ml
or 4 packets of stevia	
ice cubes	

In a pitcher, combine water, lemon (or lime) juice, and stevia. Stir until stevia dissolves. Add more stevia in very small increments if you like it a little sweeter. Serve over ice or chill till serving time.

Makes 5 servings

NUTRITIONAL FACTS PER SERVING: 4G CARBOHYDRATE; 12 CALORIES; TRACE PROTEIN • FOOD EXCHANGES: ½ FRUIT

Old-Fashioned Soda Pop

Makes ten 12-ounce bottles

1 gallon water	3.75 liters
1 teaspoon stevioside	5 ml
or 7 teaspoons stevia blend	35 ml
or 14 packets of stevia	
1 tablespoon soda pop extract	15 ml
2 tablespoons sugar	30 ml
¼ teaspoon yeast	1.25 ml

There are two ways to do this:

TRADITIONAL METHOD:

In a cup of warm water, dissolve yeast (you can use wine or beer yeast and even bread yeast but champagne yeast gives a better taste). Let stand for 5 minutes or longer to dissolve.

Combine extract with warm water, sugar, and stevioside. Stir well to dissolve sugar and stevioside. Add yeast mixture. You can taste the mixture to make adjustments to sweetness and flavor.

Sterilize bottles in boiling water. Gently pour mixture into each bottle until 1-2 inches from top. Top each bottle with caps (follow manufacturer's instructions for preparing caps).

Place bottles in a warm area, 75 to 85°F, for 3 to 4 days. Check carbonation and if satisfactory, place bottles into the refrigerator to stop carbonation process and to chill the drink. If carbonation is not yet satisfactory, allow bottles to sit in a warm area for another day or two, check carbonation, and if okay, chill. When serving, try not to disturb the yeast that will have settled to the bottom of the bottle. Most people do not like that "yeasty" taste in their beverage.

Experimenting: Most soda pop flavorings can be purchased at any home brewing supply store. This will allow you to try different flavors and mix them. One favorite is cherry coke, which is simply a mixture of the cola extract with the cherry extract.

Caution: depending on the temperature, the carbonation process may be fast or slow so be careful because the bottles could pop if it is too fast. Since the sugar content is low with this recipe, the carbonation process is limited due to a lack of food for the yeast.

Note on sugar: If you are wondering why there is a need for sugar, the answer is simple. Carbonation is achieved when the yeast turns the sugar into alcohol and carbon dioxide. Fortunately, due to the low sugar content and the short carbonation period, the beverage will have virtually no alcohol but lots of bubbles. Also, the yeast will consume the sugar during the process of carbonating the water. Since stevia is not a sugar, the yeast will ignore it and when all of the sugar is consumed, the yeast will die off.

Modern Method:

You will need to purchase a 5-gallon soda fountain container. Some home brewery supply stores carry these. Clean and sterilize the container and replace all gaskets (if purchased used). Add 5 tablespoons of the soda extract with 5 teaspoons of stevioside. Add 5 gallons of water and mix well. Seal the container and connect a CO_2 canister to the soda container. Open the CO_2 valve to give 5 pounds pressure. Bleed the soda container for about 3-4 seconds just to remove any air. Then increase the pressure to 20 pounds. Shake the soda container back and forth to force the CO_2 into the liquid. You will hear the air flow during shaking. Shake for about 5 minutes. Remove the gas line from the CO_2 tank and shut off. Allow the soda container to sit for about a day. Connect a dispensing hose and serve over ice.

This method is a bit more expensive at first because of the investment in hardware. Try the traditional method first. If you would like to then try the modern method, talk with a salesperson at your local home brewery supply store. PLEASE FOLLOW ALL MANUFACTURERS WARNINGS. YOU ARE DEALING WITH HIGH PRESSURE AND IT CAN BE DANGEROUS.

NUTRITIONAL FACTS PER SERVING: 1G CARBOHYDRATE; 4 CALORIES; TRACE TOTAL FAT; TRACE PROTEIN • FOOD EXCHANGES: 0 EXCHANGES

Quick & Easy Soda Pop

Simple and easy to keep around the office.

1 teaspoon stevia liquid	5 ml
1 cup Canada Dry Sparkling Water® (any flavor)	235 ml

Place the stevia liquid on the bottom of a glass. Add ice. Pour 1 cup of Canada Dry Sparkling Water over the ice, any flavor that you want. Adjust stevia liquid to personal taste.

Makes 1 serving

NUTRITIONAL FACTS PER SERVING: 0 NUTRITION • FOOD EXCHANGES: 0 EXCHANGES

Orange Dream Shake

½ cup milk	120 ml
½ teaspoon orange extract	2.5 ml
⅛ teaspoon stevioside	½ ml
or 1 teaspoon stevia blend	5 ml
or 2 packets of stevia	
3 tablespoons protein powder, unsweetened	45 ml
½ cup whipping cream	120 ml
6 ice cubes	6

In a blender, place milk, extract and stevioside. While blending on a medium setting, slowly add protein powder. Add cream. Finally add ice cubes 1 at a time until well crushed. Serve cold.

Makes 1 serving

NUTRITIONAL FACTS PER SERVING: 9G CARBOHYDRATE; 488 CALORIES; 48G TOTAL FAT; 6G PROTEIN • FOOD EXCHANGES: 9½ FAT

Pineapple-Peach Frappé

½ cup pineapple, water-packed	120 ml
½ cup pineapple juice, unsweetened	120 ml
2 peach halves in water	2
1 cup yogurt	235 ml
1 cup milk	235 ml
¼ teaspoon stevioside	1.25 ml
or 2 teaspoons stevia blend	20 ml
or 4 packets of stevia	
3 tablespoons protein powder 4	5 ml

Combine pineapple, juice, and peaches in container of an electric blender or food processor; process until pureed. Add yogurt, milk, stevia and protein powder; continue to process until smooth and thickened. Pour into individual glasses, and serve immediately.

Makes 6 servings

NUTRITIONAL FACTS PER SERVING: 10G CARBOHYDRATE; 76 CALORIES; 3G TOTAL FAT; 9G PROTEIN • FOOD EXCHANGES: ½ FRUIT; ½ FAT

Frappucino

2 tablespoons instant coffee powder	30 ml
½ cup water	120 ml
¼ teaspoon stevioside	1.25 ml
or 2 teaspoons stevia blend	10 ml
or 4 packets of stevia	
½ cup evaporated milk	120 ml
2 cups ice cubes	½ liter

Prepare coffee by dissolving the coffee in hot water. Allow the coffee to cool to room temperature. Combine coffee mixture, stevia, evaporated milk and ice in blender. Blend on high until no visible chunks of ice are left. Serve immediately.

Makes two 1½-cup servings

NUTRITIONAL FACTS PER SERVING: 9G CARBOHYDRATE; 98 CALORIES; 5G TOTAL FAT; 5G PROTEIN • FOOD EXCHANGES: 1 FAT

Basic Protein Shake

⅓ cup cold water	80 ml
⅓ cup heavy cream	80 ml
3 tablespoons isolated soy protein	45 ml
⅛ teaspoon stevioside	½ ml
or 1 teaspoon stevia blend	5 ml
or 2 packets of stevia ice cubes	

In a blender, combine all ingredients together and mix well. Add ice cubes until the shake has the consistency of a thick milk shake.

VARIATIONS:

This is the base for an infinite number of variations. Use your favorite extract, add fruit, nuts, etc., whatever you want, but you have to keep in mind that everything that you add to this basic recipe adds carbs. So be careful but have fun.

Makes 1 serving

NUTRITIONAL FACTS PER SERVING: 2G CARBOHYDRATE; 426 CALORIES; 29G TOTAL FAT; 41G PROTEIN • FOOD EXCHANGES: 6 FAT

7

Breads, Breakfasts and Protein Bars

Breads, Breakfasts and Protein Bars

Baking Mix

2 cups soy flour	475 ml
4 cups soy protein isolate	950 ml
4 tablespoons baking soda	60 ml
2 teaspoons stevia blend	10ml
2 teaspoons salt	10 ml

In a food processor, blend all ingredients together. Store in an airtight container.

Makes twenty-five ¼-cup servings

NUTRITIONAL FACTS PER SERVING: 2G CARBOHYDRATE; 169 CALORIES; 2G TOTAL FAT; 37G PROTEIN • FOOD EXCHANGES: ½ LEAN MEAT

Cheese Rolls

1 cup Baking Mix	235 ml
½ teaspoon salt	2.5 ml
1 teaspoon garlic powder	5 ml
¼ cup butter	60 ml
2 tablespoons heavy cream	30 ml
½ cup seltzer water	120 ml
3 tablespoons sour cream	45 ml
1 ounce parmesan cheese	28 g
2 ounces cheddar cheese	56 g

In a large bowl, mix first three ingredients together. Cut in butter to make a crumbly mix. Stir in cream, seltzer water and sour cream to form dough. Knead in cheeses. Spoon onto cookie sheet and bake at 350°F for 15-20 minutes.

Variation: Add two finely chopped jalapeños for added spice.

Makes 12 rolls

NUTRITIONAL FACTS PER SERVING: 9G CARBOHYDRATE; 433 CALORIES; 11G TOTAL FAT; 79G PROTEIN • FOOD EXCHANGES: ½ STARCH; 1 LEAN MEAT; 1½ FAT

Protein Bread

Reminiscent of corn bread in flavor

3 eggs, separated	3
2 tablespoons butter, melted	30 ml
2 tablespoons sour cream	30 ml
½ cup soya powder	120 ml
1 tablespoon baking powder	15 ml

In a large bowl, combine egg yolks with remaining ingredients until well incorporated. In a separate bowl, whip egg whites until stiff and then fold into egg yolk mixture. Pour into a greased bread pan and bake in a pre-heated oven at 350 degrees for 50 minutes.

Makes 6 slices

PER SERVING: 3G CARBOHYDRATE; 111 CALORIES; 9G TOTAL FAT; 6G PROTEIN • FOOD EXCHANGES: ½ LEAN MEAT; 1 FAT

Low-Carb Tortillas

Try these hot off the griddle, with a dab of butter – Delicious!

⅔ cup rolled oat flour	158 ml
1 teaspoon salt	5 ml
3 tablespoons shortening	45 ml
2 teaspoons baking powder	10 ml
1½ cups soy protein isolate	355 ml
⅔ cup wheat gluten	158 ml

Mix all ingredients together. Add water as needed to make dough that is pliable but not sticky. Roll dough into balls, the size of a lemon. Place a ball between two sheets of wax paper. Roll out to 3-4 inches. Grill on a lightly greased skillet until lightly brown and crispy on both sides.

Makes 20, 3-inch tortillas

NUTRITIONAL FACTS PER SERVING: 8G CARBOHYDRATE; 113 CALORIES; 4G TOTAL FAT; 12G PROTEIN; 2G DIETARY FIBER • FOOD EXCHANGES: 1 LEAN MEAT; 1/2 FAT

Orange Chocolate Muffins

⅔ cup oil	160 ml
1 cup water	235 ml
⅓ cup heavy cream	80 ml
3 eggs	3
1 teaspoon vanilla	5 ml
½ teaspoon stevioside	2.5 ml
or 4 teaspoons stevia blend	20 ml
or 8 packets of stevia	
1 cup whey protein	235 ml
2 tablespoons rolled oat flour	30 ml
2 tablespoons wheat gluten	30 ml
2 teaspoons baking powder	10 ml
¼ cup cocoa powder	60 ml
2 teaspoons orange peel	10 ml
¼ cup chopped walnuts	60 ml

In a mixer, combine oil, water, cream, eggs, vanilla and stevia. Blend well. Add remaining ingredients except nuts. Once the muffin mix is well incorporated, fold in nuts. Pour into greased muffin tins and bake at 350 degrees for 10 to 15 minutes. Remove and allow to cool.

Makes 12 muffins

PER SERVING: 5G CARBOHYDRATE; 256 CALORIES; 18G TOTAL FAT; 22G PROTEIN • FOOD EXCHANGES: ½ LEAN MEAT; 3½ FAT;

Pumpkin Muffins

1 cup whey protein	235 ml
¼ cup rolled oat flour	60 ml
2 teaspoons baking powder	10 ml
1 teaspoon baking soda	5 ml
½ teaspoon nutmeg	2.5 ml
1 teaspoon cinnamon	5 ml
½ teaspoon stevioside	2.5 ml
or 4 teaspoons stevia blend	20 ml
or 8 packets of stevia	
1 egg	1
½ cup oil	120 ml
¼ cup canned pumpkin	60 ml
2 tablespoons heavy cream	30 ml
¼ cup water	60 ml

In a large mixing bowl, combine first seven ingredients. In a separate bowl, mix remaining ingredients well. Combine wet ingredients with dry ingredients and mix until well incorporated. Pour batter into greased muffin tins and bake at 350 degrees for 15 to 20 minutes or until centers are firm and bounce back when slightly touched. Serve with whipped cream.

Makes 12 muffins

PER SERVING: 5G CARBOHYDRATE; 185 CALORIES; 11G TOTAL FAT; 18G PROTEIN •
FOOD EXCHANGES: 2 FAT

Pancakes

½ cup Baking Mix (see Index)	120 ml
⅛ teaspoon stevioside	½ ml
or 1 teaspoon stevia blend	5 ml
or 2 packets of stevia	
2 eggs	2
1 tablespoon heavy cream	5 ml
⅓ cup seltzer water	80 ml
2 tablespoons oil, for frying	30 ml

In a medium bowl, mix all ingredients, except oil, well. In a skillet, heat 2 tablespoons of oil over medium heat. Spoon batter onto skillet making 3-inch pancakes. Cook for about 3-4 minutes or until bottom of pancake is golden brown. Turn pancakes over and cook other side until golden brown. Remove and serve hot.

Makes 5 servings (about 10 x 3 inch pancakes)

PER SERVING: 1G CARBOHYDRATE; 85 CALORIES; 8G TOTAL FAT; 2G PROTEIN • FOOD EXCHANGES: ½ LEAN MEAT; 1½ FAT

VARIATION:

Waffles: To make waffles, separate eggs. Whip egg whites until stiff peaks form. Add egg yolks to other ingredients and mix well. Fold egg whites into egg yolk mixture. Grease waffle iron well and add a heaping spoonful of batter to each waffle iron. Close and cook until golden brown. Serve hot with butter, whipped cream, and fresh fruit.

Crepes

2 large eggs	2
⅔ cup milk	160 ml
1 tablespoon butter, melted	15 ml
½ cup soy flour	120 ml
⅛ teaspoon stevioside	½ ml
or 1 teaspoon stevia blend	5 ml
or 2 packets of stevia	
¼ teaspoon salt	1.25 ml
vegetable oil	

Beat eggs thoroughly. Blend in milk and melted butter. Stir in flour, stevia and salt only until smooth. Lightly brush a 5-inch crepe pan with oil. (Use a larger size pan for larger crepes.) Heat over medium heat. Pour in 2 tablespoons of batter and tilt pan carefully so batter covers entire bottom of pan. Cook 2 minutes on each side or until golden brown. Repeat with remaining mixture, oiling pan if needed.

Makes about 12 crepes

PER SERVING: 2G CARBOHYDRATE; 45 CALORIES; 3G TOTAL FAT; 3G PROTEIN • FOOD EXCHANGES: ½ LEAN MEAT; ½ FAT

Cheese Blintzes

A great way to start the day

2 cups ricotta cheese	475 ml
3 ounces cream cheese	85 g
1 teaspoon vanilla	5 ml
⅜ teaspoon stevioside	1.8 ml
or 3 teaspoons stevia blend	15 ml
or 6 packets of stevia	
12 crepes (see Index)	12

In a mixer, combine ricotta cheese, cream cheese, vanilla and stevia and blend well. Place in refrigerator until needed.

Prepare crepes as instructed in recipe. Place a piece of wax paper between crepes to prevent sticking. When all 12 crepes are finished, place 2 heaping spoonfuls of the cheese mixture onto each crepe and roll the crepe tightly. Serve with a dab of sour cream and fresh fruit.

Makes 12 blintzes

PER SERVING: 4G CARBOHYDRATE; 142 CALORIES; 11G TOTAL FAT; 8G PROTEIN • FOOD EXCHANGES: 1 LEAN MEAT; 1½ FAT

Protein Bars
On-The-Go Energy

Store bought protein bars are a great time saver and taste delicious. Unfortunately, at around $2.00 each, they can quickly deplete most people's budget. Don't despair—some inexpensive alternatives are the following protein bars. Although they are similar to the commercial protein bars, they certainly aren't exact copies. The differences are because many of the ingredients in store bought bars are only available commercially. Fortunately, these home made bars are very good, fill you up on-the-go and will save you money.

Best Brownie Protein Bars

½ cup oat flour	118 ml
¼ cup whole-wheat flour	59 ml
1 cup whey protein powder	237 ml
½ cup stevia blend	118 ml
⅓ cup cocoa	79 ml
¼ teaspoon baking powder	1.25 ml
¼ teaspoon salt	1.25 ml
1 tablespoon liquid lecithin	15 ml
½ cup fat free cream cheese (room temperature)	118 ml
2 eggs	2 each
¼ cup fat free Miracle Whip	59 ml
1 teaspoon super-strength chocolate flavoring (LorAnn®)	5 ml

Preheat oven to 325°F. Line a 9"x9" baking pan with wax paper.

In a bowl combine all dry ingredients. Set aside. In a large bowl, with an electric beater, combine lecithin, cream cheese, eggs, Miracle Whip, and flavoring until light and fluffy. Add the dry ingredients to the wet. Mix well. Pour batter into lined 9"x9" square pan and smooth evenly.

Bake for 15-20 minutes. Remove from pan and cool slightly. Remove wax paper and cool completely. Cut into 9 bars.

Makes 9 servings.

NUTRITIONAL FACTS PER SERVING; 9 G CARBOHYDRATE, 99 CALORIES; 3 G TOTAL FAT; 9 G PROTEIN

Chewy Chocolate Peanut Butter Protein Bars

1 cup oat flour	237 ml
1½ cups whey protein powder	355 ml
¼ cup cocoa powder	25 ml
½ cup nonfat dry milk powder	118 ml
¼ cup stevia blend	59 ml
½ teaspoon salt	2.5 ml
2 egg whites	2 each
½ teaspoon super-strength chocolate flavoring (LorAnn)	2.5 ml
½ teaspoon super-strength peanut butter flavoring (LorAnn)	2.5 ml
¼ cup creamy peanut butter	59 ml
¼–⅓ cup water	59–79 ml

Preheat oven to 325°F. Line a 9"x9" baking pan with wax paper.

Combine all dry ingredients in blender—Process on high speed 2 minutes. In a bowl, beat eggs, flavorings, and peanut butter. Add the dry ingredients to the egg mixture. With an electric mixer, slowly add the water until dough becomes a "gooey play-dough" consistency. Pour batter in lined pan, spreading, or pressing dough to an even thickness.

Bake for about 15 minutes. Remove from pan and allow to cool slightly. Remove wax paper and allow to cool completely. Cut into 8 bars. Delicious with low-carb ice cream.

Makes 8 servings.

NUTRITIONAL FACTS PER SERVING; 24G CARBOHYDRATE, 250 CALORIES; 7G TOTAL FAT; 24G PROTEIN

Almond Bars

TASTES LIKE MARZIPAN!

2 cups almond meal	473 ml
½ cup Fearn Soya Powder®	118 ml
¼ cup stevia blend	59 ml
½ cup salted butter—room temperature	118 ml
2 eggs	2 each
⅛ teaspoon almond oil super-strength flavoring (LorAnn)	.6 ml
1 cup slivered almonds	277 ml

Preheat oven to 300º F. Lightly grease a 9"x9" pan.

In the container of a food processor, combine almond meal, Soya Powder, and stevia blend. Process until well combined. Add the butter, eggs, and flavoring—Process on high for 3 minutes. Add the slivered almonds and process until just combined. The dough should be the consistency of very sticky cookie dough. Add more Soya Powder one tablespoon at a time if needed. To prevent sticking, lightly butter fingers and press into prepared 9"x9" pan. Cook at 300 for 12 minutes or until edges are golden. Remove from pan onto cooling rack. After cool, cut into 14 bars with a sharp knife.

Makes 14 servings

NUTRITIONAL FACTS PER SERVING; 9G CARBOHYDRATE, 223CALORIES; 17G TOTAL FAT; 12G PROTEIN

Coconut Protein Bars

ECONOMICAL, AND DELICIOUS!

½ cup plus 2 tablespoons water	145 ml
or ¼ cup Stevia blend	59 ml
or ¾ teaspoon pure stevia (stevioside)	4 ml
⅓ cup glycerin	79 ml
2 tablespoons coconut oil	30 ml

½ teaspoon coconut super-strength flavoring (LorAnn Brand)	2.5 ml
½ teaspoon pineapple super-strength flavoring (LorAnn Brand)	2.5 ml
1½ cups isolated soy protein powder	355 ml
¾ cup Milk & Egg Protein powder (MLO®)	177 ml
½ cup unsweetened shredded coconut (dried, NOT fresh)	118 ml

In a microwave safe container, heat ½ cup of water to a boil; dissolve stevia in hot water. Add glycerin, coconut oil and extracts to water mixture—Set aside to cool completely. Add flavorings. (Warm or hot water will ruin the texture of this protein bar.)

Next, in a mixing bowl or large food processor container combine soy protein, Milk and Egg protein (MLO), and coconut. Slowly pour the cooled water mixture into the dry mixture and process with a sturdy mixer or food processor until the dough forms coarse crumbs. Leaving the mixture in bowl, kneed it into a large ball. It should be the consistency of pie pastry dough, firm, yet slightly crumbly. If it is sticky, add more soy protein powder. If the dough is not moist enough to hold together when you squeeze it add more water one tablespoon at a time.

Finally, forming the protein bars is essential to giving them that "store bought taste". Press the dough evenly into a slightly oiled 8"x8" pan. Lightly oil the top of the dough. Place another 8" x 8" pan on top of the dough. Place weights on top of this pan. (I use 50 pounds worth of hand weights.) Allow the dough to press for several hours or longer depending on your personal taste. Alternative method: Press dough onto a cooking sheet into an 8" x 8" square. Using heavy meat pounder or rolling pin, pound the dough until desired textured. After pressing the dough, cut into bars 1½" x 4". Makes about 12 bars. These bars contain no preservatives so they must be refrigerated for storage.

NUTRITIONAL FACTS PER SERVING; 2 G CARBOHYDRATE, 100 CALORIES; 5 G TOTAL FAT; 11 G PROTEIN

Chocolate Raspberry Protein Bars

1 cup oat flour	237 ml
1 cup Milk & Egg Protein powder (MLO®)	237 ml
½ cup powdered milk	118 ml
½ teaspoon pure stevioside extract	2.5 ml
½ teaspoon salt	2.5 ml
2 ounces unsweetened bakers chocolate	60 g
2 tablespoons butter	30 ml
8 ounces fat free cream cheese (room temperature)	226 ml
½ cup glycerin	118 ml
1 teaspoon super-strength chocolate flavoring (LorAnn®)	5 ml

Preheat oven to 325°. Line a 8½"x11" baking pan with wax paper.

Combine all dry ingredients in blender—Process on high speed 2 minutes. Set aside. Using a double boiler, melt chocolate and butter. In a bowl, beat cream cheese, glycerin, and flavoring and melted chocolate mixture. Using an electric mixer, add the dry ingredients to the wet mixture. Pour batter into lined pan, spreading to an even thickness.

Bake for about 20 minutes. Remove from pan and allow to cool slightly. Remove wax paper and allow to cool completely. Cut into 8 bars.

Makes 8 servings

NUTRITIONAL FACTS PER SERVING; 27 G CARBOHYDRATE, 364 CALORIES; 14 G TOTAL FAT; 34 G PROTEIN

8

Soups, Salads and Dressings

Soups, Salads and Dressings

Pumpkin Soup

1 pumpkin (about 3 pounds)	1 (6.6 kg)
1 cup onion, chopped	235 ml
½ cup celery, chopped	120 ml
4 tablespoons butter, melted	60 ml
4 cups chicken broth	1 liter
salt & pepper	

To prepare pumpkin: Preheat oven to 350 degrees. Slice pumpkin in half vertically and remove all seeds and stringy material. Place the pumpkin in a baking dish, cut sides down. Add about ½ inch of water. Bake for 1 hour or until tender. Cut each pumpkin half into strips and then remove peel. Place peeled pumpkin into a bowl.

In a large saucepan, sauté onion and celery in butter until onions are clear. In a food processor, place pumpkin with sautéed vegetables and 1 cup of chicken broth. Puree until smooth. Return to saucepan and add remaining chicken broth and simmer. Salt and pepper to taste.

Makes 8 servings

NUTRITIONAL FACTS PER SERVING: 3G CARBOHYDRATE; 83 CALORIES; 6G TOTAL FAT; 3G PROTEIN • FOOD EXCHANGES: ½ VEGETABLE; 1 FAT

Variation: Curried Pumpkin Soup

2 cups heavy cream	470 ml
½ teaspoon curry powder (see Index)	5 ml
⅛ teaspoon stevioside	½ ml
or 1 teaspoon stevia blend	5 ml
or 2 packets of stevia	
¼ cup parsley, minced	60 ml
½ cup pumpkin seeds, roasted	120 ml

Follow the directions above for the pumpkin soup through point at which pumpkin is pureed, then add heavy cream, curry powder and stevia. Return soup to saucepan, add remaining chicken broth and simmer for 15 minutes. After the soup has simmered, pour into bowls and garnish with minced parsley and roasted pumpkin seeds.

Makes 10 Servings

NUTRITIONAL FACTS PER SERVING: 6G CARBOHYDRATE; 245 CALORIES; 23G TOTAL FAT; 4G PROTEIN • FOOD EXCHANGES: ½ VEGETABLE; 4 ½ FAT

Herb & Lamb Stew

½ cup red beans	120 ml
4 tablespoons olive oil	60 ml
1 onion, diced	1
1 pound lamb, cubed	455 g
¼ cup lime juice	60 ml
⅛ teaspoon stevioside	½ ml
or 1 teaspoon stevia blend	5 ml
or 2 packets of stevia	
3 cups water	710 ml
1 cup finely chopped fresh parsley	235 ml
½ cup finely chopped fresh scallions	120 ml
½ cup finely chopped leeks	120 ml
salt and pepper	
⅓ cup dry white wine	80 ml

Soak the beans overnight until soft. Drain and rinse the beans and then set them aside. In a large skillet, heat oil over medium heat and sauté onion until clear. Add lamb and brown meat well. Add the beans to the meat with limejuice and stevia. Salt and pepper to taste.

Transfer meat to a stockpot and add water. Cover and simmer for 1 hour. Gently sauté vegetables in skillet with 1 tablespoon of oil until leeks are tender, about 5-6 minutes. Add herbs and white wine and simmer for 5 minutes more. Stir leek mixture into meat and gently simmer for 30 minutes. Season to taste.

Makes 8 servings

NUTRITIONAL FACTS PER SERVING: 11G CARBOHYDRATE; 231 CALORIES; 16G TOTAL FAT; 11G PROTEIN • FOOD EXCHANGES: ½ STARCH; 1 LEAN MEAT; ½ VEGETABLE; 2½ FAT

Sauerkraut Soup

1 pound sauerkraut	455 g
4 cups beef broth	950 ml
2 pounds pork spareribs	900 g
2 bay leaves	2
8 peppercorns	8
2 ounces dried mushrooms	60 g
4 cups water	950 ml
⅜ teaspoon stevioside	1.8 ml
or 3 teaspoons stevia blend	15 ml
or 6 packets of stevia	
salt and pepper	

Rinse sauerkraut lightly in cold water. Drain and set aside. In a large pot, place beef broth, spareribs, bay leaves, peppercorns and mushrooms. Cover and cook for 90 minutes or until meat is done. Remove mushrooms and cut into strips, then return to pot. Add water, sauerkraut and stevia to the pot. Cover and cook for 30 minutes. Remove pork, cut meat off the bones, slice the meat into strips 1-inch long and then return to pot. Salt and pepper to taste.

Makes 8 servings

NUTRITIONAL FACTS PER SERVING: 10G CARBOHYDRATE; 263 CALORIES; 17G TOTAL FAT; 19G PROTEIN • FOOD EXCHANGES: 2½ LEAN MEAT; 1½ VEGETABLE; 2½ FAT

Mushroom Soup

16 ounces mushrooms	455 g
¼ cup lemon juice	60 ml
2 onions, finely chopped	2
2 tablespoons butter	30 ml
½ cup water	120 ml
6 cups beef stock	1,425 ml
1 cup sour cream	235 ml
⅛ teaspoon stevioside	½ ml
or 1 teaspoon stevia blend	5 ml
or 2 packets of stevia	
salt and pepper	
finely chopped parsley or dill	

Wash mushrooms in a cold water bath with lemon juice. Thinly slice mushrooms. Sauté mushrooms and onions in butter until they're cooked through and soft. Add water and then transfer to soup kettle with beef stock. In a separate bowl, blend sour cream and stevia with 1 cup of broth until lump free. Add to kettle and allow to simmer for 10 minutes. Salt and pepper to taste. Garnish with chopped dill or parsley.

Makes about 6 servings.

NUTRITIONAL FACTS PER SERVING: 9G CARBOHYDRATE; 186 CALORIES; 14G TOTAL FAT; 4G PROTEIN • FOOD EXCHANGES: 1½ VEGETABLE; 3 FAT

Egg Drop Soup

4 cups chicken broth	950 ml
¼ cup water	60 ml
1 teaspoon soy sauce	5 ml
½ teaspoon stevioside	2.5 ml
or 4 teaspoons stevia blend	20 ml
or 8 packets of stevia	
½ teaspoon lemon juice	2.5 ml
2 eggs	2
salt & pepper	
1 scallion, for garnish	1

Bring chicken broth and water to a boil. Add soy sauce and stevia.

Beat eggs well and set aside. With the mixture still boiling, slowly add the egg, stirring constantly. Add lemon juice(if you would like a little zip in this soup). Salt and pepper to taste, spoon into bowls and garnish with chopped scallions.

Makes 4 servings

NUTRITIONAL FACTS PER SERVING: 2G CARBOHYDRATE; 58 CALORIES; 2G TOTAL FAT; 4G PROTEIN • FOOD EXCHANGES: ½ LEAN MEAT

Beet Borsch

4 beets	4
1 apple, peeled & grated	1
6 cups beef stock	1525 ml
¼ cup dry red wine	60 ml
1 bay leaf, crumbled	1
¼ teaspoon stevioside	1.25 ml
or 2 teaspoons stevia blend	10 ml
or 4 packets of stevia	
¼ teaspoon marjoram	1.25 ml
3 tablespoons raisins, optional	45 ml
1 lemon	1
salt and pepper	

Bake beets in a 375-degree oven until tender. Allow to cool and then peel and grate the beets. Place in a soup kettle with apple and beef stock. Bring to a boil. Add red wine, bay leaf, stevia, marjoram. Allow soup to simmer for 10 minutes and then strain. Add raisins to strained broth and let simmer for another 5 minutes. Remove raisins and squeeze in lemon juice and salt and pepper to taste.

Makes 8 servings

NUTRITIONAL FACTS PER SERVING: 11G CARBOHYDRATE; 62 CALORIES; TRACE TOTAL FAT; 2G PROTEIN • FOOD EXCHANGES: 1 VEGETABLE; ½ FRUIT

Avocado Soup

2 each avocados	2 each
½ teaspoon lemon juice	2.5 ml
2 cups chicken broth	475 ml
⅛ teaspoon stevioside	½ ml
or 1 teaspoon stevia blend	5 ml
or 2 packets of stevia	
1 cup heavy cream	235 ml
2 tablespoons dry sherry	30 ml
salt & cayenne pepper to taste	

Peel and pit avocados. Place avocado meat into a blender or food processor and puree with the lemon juice. Blend in chicken broth, stevia and sherry. Pour into a bowl and whisk in cream. Season to taste with salt and cayenne pepper. Serve chilled.

Makes approximately four 1-cup servings

NUTRITIONAL FACTS PER SERVING: 10G CARBOHYDRATE; 395 CALORIES; 38G TOTAL FAT; 6G PROTEIN • FOOD EXCHANGES: ½ FRUIT; 7½ FAT

Mock Potato Salad

1 head cauliflower	1 head
1 cup mayonnaise	240 ml
1 cup sour cream	240 ml
1 teaspoon mustard powder	5 ml
1 teaspoon salt	5 ml
1 teaspoon pepper	5 ml
½ cup refrigerator sweet pickles	120 ml
½ cup onion, diced	120 ml
⅛ teaspoon stevioside	½ ml
or 1 teaspoon stevia blend	5 ml
or 2 packets of stevia	
¼ cup chives	60 ml
2 slices cooked bacon, crumbled	2 slices
6 eggs, hard-boiled, sliced	6

Remove leaves and stem of cauliflower and then wash the cauliflower well. Cut into florets. Steam or microwave the florets until tender but not soft. Set aside and allow florets to cool.

In a large bowl, combine mayonnaise, sour cream, mustard powder, salt, pepper, chopped pickles, onion, stevioside and chives. Mix well. Add cooked cauliflower and coat well. Place into a serving bowl, garnish with bacon and sliced eggs.

Makes 8 servings

NUTRITIONAL FACTS PER SERVING: 3G CARBOHYDRATE; 335 CALORIES; 34G TOTAL FAT; 7G PROTEIN • FOOD EXCHANGES: ½ LEAN MEAT; ½ VEGETABLE; 3½ FAT

Marinated Turkey–Tomato Pasta Salad

1 medium red onion, thinly sliced	1 medium
16 cherry tomatoes, quartered	16
1½ cups turkey, chopped	355 g
2 cups iceberg lettuce, thinly sliced	475 ml
⅓ cup fresh basil, chopped	80 ml
⅛ teaspoon stevioside	½ ml
1 teaspoon stevia blend	5 ml
or 2 packets of stevia	
¼ cup balsamic vinegar	60 ml
3 tablespoons olive oil	45 ml
salt and pepper	
protein pasta (see Index)	

In a large bowl, toss all ingredients except pasta and salt & pepper. Cook pasta according to recipe instructions. Allow pasta to cool and then add and toss with turkey mix. Salt and pepper to taste.

Makes 4 servings

NUTRITIONAL FACTS PER SERVING: 8G CARBOHYDRATE; 238 CALORIES; 16G TOTAL FAT; 16G PROTEIN • FOOD EXCHANGES: 2 LEAN MEAT; 1½ VEGETABLE; 2 FAT

German Mock Potato Salad

1 head cauliflower	1 head
6 slices bacon	6 slices
½ cup onion, chopped	120 ml
¼ cup celery, sliced	60 ml
1 tablespoon olive oil	15 ml
1 teaspoon salt	5 ml
½ teaspoon celery seed	2.5 ml
⅛ teaspoon pepper	½ ml
¼ teaspoon stevioside	1.25 ml
or 2 teaspoons stevia blend	10 ml
or 4 packets of stevia	
¼ cup apple cider vinegar	60 ml
½ cup water	120 ml
3 eggs, hard-boiled	3

Remove leaves from cauliflower and wash cauliflower well. Cut cauliflower into florets. Steam or microwave the florets until tender but not soft. Set aside and allow to cool.

DRESSING:

In a frying pan, cook bacon slices until crisp. Drain and crumble; set aside. Cook onion and celery in olive oil till tender. Stir in salt, celery seed, and pepper. In a glass or measuring cup, dissolve stevia into the vinegar. Add vinegar and water to onions. Stirring constantly, cook until thick and bubbly. Remove from heat. In a large bowl, add cauliflower and bacon and pour vinaigrette over the cauliflower. Mix until well coated. Spoon mixture into a serving bowl, and garnish with sliced hard-boiled eggs and crumbled bacon.

Makes 6 servings

NUTRITIONAL FACTS PER SERVING: 3G CARBOHYDRATE; 107 CALORIES; 8G TOTAL FAT; 6G PROTEIN • FOOD EXCHANGES: ½ LEAN MEAT; ½ VEGETABLE; 1 FAT

Crab Pasta Salad

1 pound crab meat	455 g
½ cup scallion, chopped	120 ml
¼ teaspoon white pepper	1.25 ml
2 tablespoons capers, drained	30 ml
juice of 1 lime	1
½ teaspoon salt	2.5 ml
½ cup celery, chopped	120 ml
1 teaspoon dill	5 ml
1 ounce parmesan cheese, shredded	60 g
⅛ teaspoon stevioside	½ ml
or 1 teaspoon stevia blend	5 ml
or 2 packets of stevia	
protein pasta (see Index)	

Prepare pasta as per recipe instructions. Allow pasta to cool.

In a large bowl, combine remaining ingredients and mix well. Add pasta and toss. Refrigerate for about 2 hours to allow flavors to blend.

Makes 4 servings

NUTRITIONAL FACTS PER SERVING: 4G CARBOHYDRATE; 190 CALORIES; 6G TOTAL FAT; 30G PROTEIN • FOOD EXCHANGES: 4 LEAN MEAT; ½ VEGETABLE; ½ FAT

Creamy Coleslaw

1 cup mayonnaise	235 ml
3 teaspoons cider vinegar	15 ml
⅛ teaspoon stevioside	½ ml
or 1 teaspoon stevia blend	5 ml
or 2 packets of stevia	
¼ teaspoon celery seeds	1.25 ml
¼ teaspoon salt	1.25 ml
⅛ teaspoon black pepper	½ ml
1 teaspoon onions, minced	5 ml
3 cups green cabbage, shredded	705 ml
2 cups red cabbage, shredded	470 ml
½ green bell pepper, minced	½

In a large bowl, whisk together mayonnaise, vinegar, stevia, celery seeds, salt, black pepper and onion. Set aside. In a separate bowl, mix together remaining ingredients. Pour mayonnaise mixture over cabbage mixture and toss. Serve.

Makes 6 servings

NUTRITIONAL FACTS PER SERVING: 5G CARBOHYDRATE; 283 CALORIES; 31G TOTAL FAT; 1G PROTEIN • FOOD EXCHANGES: 1 VEGETABLE; 2½ FAT

VARIATION: CAJUN COLESLAW

2 tablespoons mustard	30 ml
1 teaspoon hot sauce	5 ml
2 tablespoons traditional catsup (see index)	30 ml
1 tablespoon Worcestershire sauce	15 ml

Add these ingredients during the first step. Add an extra 2 cups shredded cabbage during the second step. Makes 10 servings for 6 carbohydrates per serving.

Avocado Dressing

1 avocado	1
½ cup lemon juice	120 ml
¼ cup mayonnaise	60 ml
⅛ teaspoon stevioside	½ ml
or 1 teaspoon stevia blend	5 ml
or 2 packets of stevia	
¼ teaspoon salt	1.25 ml
¼ teaspoon paprika	1.25 ml

In a food processor or blender, blend all ingredients together until smooth. Store in refrigerator for up to 1 week. Serve over grilled strips of meat, vegetables or as a dip for fried cheese.

NUTRITIONAL FACTS PER SERVING: 6G CARBOHYDRATE; 188 CALORIES; 19G TOTAL FAT; 1G PROTEIN • FOOD EXCHANGES: ½ FRUIT; 2½ FAT

Caesar Salad Dressing

4 ounces anchovies	115 g
3 tablespoons Dijon mustard	45 ml
2 cloves garlic, minced	2 cloves
4 egg yolks	4
½ cup red wine vinegar	120 ml
1 tablespoon Worcestershire sauce	15 ml
1 cup Parmesan cheese	235 ml
1 cup olive oil	235 ml
1 teaspoon black pepper	5 ml
to taste salt to taste	
⅛ teaspoon stevioside	½ ml
or 1 teaspoon stevia blend	5 ml
or 2 packets of stevia	

In a food processor, puree all ingredients (add additional olive oil if needed to ensure proper flow of dressing). Chill in refrigerator for about 1 hour to allow flavors to blend. Toss with romaine lettuce and Parmesan cheese if you want a Caesar salad.

Variation: Grill a chicken breast and then place on top of the Caesar salad. Drizzle extra dressing over chicken and garnish with extra Parmesan cheese.

Makes 12 servings

NUTRITIONAL FACTS PER SERVING: 3G CARBOHYDRATE; 241 CALORIES; 23G TOTAL FAT; 7G PROTEIN • FOOD EXCHANGES: 1 LEAN MEAT; ½ VEGETABLE; 4 FAT

Dijon Vinaigrette

½ cup olive oil	120 ml
½ teaspoon paprika	2.5 ml
⅛ teaspoon stevioside	½ ml
or 1 teaspoon stevia blend	5 ml
or 2 packets of stevia	
¼ cup Dijon mustard	60 ml
¼ cup balsamic vinegar	60 ml
1 clove garlic, minced	1 clove
¼ teaspoon pepper	1.25 ml

In a screw-top jar, combine all ingredients. Cover, shake well. Keeps in the refrigerator for up to 1 week. Shake well before serving.

Yield: four ¼-cup servings

NUTRITIONAL FACTS PER SERVING: 2G CARBOHYDRATE; 255 CALORIES; 28G TOTAL FAT; 1G PROTEIN • FOOD EXCHANGES: 5½ FAT

French Dressing

6 tablespoons tarragon vinegar	90 ml
2 tablespoons lemon juice	30 ml
1 teaspoon seasoned salt	5 ml
½ teaspoon white pepper	2.5 ml
1 cup olive oil	235 ml
1 teaspoon Dijon mustard	5 ml
½ teaspoon dry mustard	2.5 ml
⅛ teaspoon stevioside	½ ml
or 1 teaspoon stevioside	5 ml
or 2 packets of stevia	

Blend all ingredients together. Store in refrigerator until needed. Stores for 1 week.

Makes 4 servings

NUTRITIONAL FACTS PER SERVING: 2G CARBOHYDRATE; 486 CALORIES; 54G TOTAL FAT; TRACE PROTEIN • FOOD EXCHANGES: 11 FAT

Italian Dressing

2 tablespoons Parmesan cheese	30 ml
⅛ teaspoon stevioside	½ ml
or 1 teaspoon stevia blend	5 ml
or 2 packets of stevia	
⅛ teaspoon salt	½ ml
⅛ teaspoon pepper	½ ml
1 tablespoon onion, minced	15 ml
3 tablespoons parsley, minced	45 ml
1 tablespoon basil, minced	15 ml
1 tablespoon marjoram, minced	15 ml
½ teaspoon celery seed	2.5 ml
1 clove garlic, minced	1 clove
⅓ cup white wine vinegar	80 ml
¾ cup olive oil	175 ml

In a screw-top jar, combine all ingredients. Cover, shake well. Keeps in the refrigerator for up to 1 week. Shake well before serving.

Yields: four ¼-cup servings

NUTRITIONAL FACTS PER SERVING: 3G CARBOHYDRATE; 380 CALORIES; 41G TOTAL FAT; 1.2G PROTEIN • FOOD EXCHANGES: 8 FAT

Poppy Seed Dressing

1 tablespoon poppy seeds	15 ml
¼ teaspoon dry mustard	1.25 ml
2 tablespoons water	30 ml
¼ teaspoon onion powder	1.25 ml
⅛ teaspoon stevioside	½ ml
or 1 teaspoon stevia blend	5 ml
or 2 packets of stevia	
2 tablespoons apple cider vinegar	30 ml
½ cup sour cream	120 ml

In a small saucepan, combine poppy seeds, mustard, water, onion powder and stevia. Heat just till boiling, stirring occasionally. Remove from heat. Allow dressing to cool slightly. Add vinegar and sour cream and mix well. Pour into an airtight container; keep refrigerated until needed, up to 5 days.

Makes about ½ cup

NUTRITIONAL FACTS PER SERVING: 9G CARBOHYDRATE; 301 CALORIES; 28G TOTAL FAT; 5G PROTEIN • FOOD EXCHANGES: 5½ FAT

Russian Dressing

½ cup mayonnaise	120 ml
½ cup sour cream	120 ml
1 tablespoon Dijon mustard	15 ml
1 tablespoon Worcestershire sauce	15 ml
2 tablespoons tomato sauce	30 ml
½ teaspoon grated onions	2.5 ml
⅛ teaspoon garlic powder	½ ml
⅛ teaspoon stevioside	½ ml
or 1 teaspoon stevia blend	5 ml
or 2 packets of stevia	

In a food processor or blender, blend all ingredients together until smooth. Store in refrigerator for up to 1 week.

Makes 1 cup (4 servings)

NUTRITIONAL FACTS PER SERVING: 3G CARBOHYDRATE; 267 CALORIES; 30G TOTAL FAT; 2G PROTEIN • FOOD EXCHANGES: 3 FAT

9

Appetizers & Side Dishes

Appetizers & Side Dishes

Protein Crisps

A low carbohydrate replacement for chips and crackers

4 tablespoons oat flour	60 ml
¼ teaspoon stevioside	1.25 ml
or 2 teaspoons stevia blend	10 ml
or 4 packets of stevia	
8 tablespoons soy protein isolate	120 ml
5 tablespoons butter	75 ml
2 egg whites	2

Blend oat flour, stevia and soy protein together in a mixer. Add soft butter and with a fork mix well until crumbly. Mix in two egg whites and mix well. Roll dough out very, very thin and cut into 18 small squares. Bake on a greased cookie tray in preheated oven at 350 degrees for 10 minutes. Remove from cookie tray and allow to cool.

Makes 18 servings

NUTRITIONAL FACTS PER SERVING: TRACE CARBOHYDRATE; 30 CALORIES; 3G TOTAL FAT; TRACE PROTEIN • FOOD EXCHANGES: ½ FAT

Texas Spiced Pecans

A nice fall snack.

¼ teaspoon nutmeg	1.25 ml
¼ teaspoon ground clove	1.25 ml
1 teaspoon cinnamon	5 ml
¾ teaspoon salt	3.7 ml
1 each egg white	1 each
2 cups pecans	475 ml
½ teaspoon stevioside	2.5 ml
or 4 teaspoons stevia blend	20 ml
or 8 packets of stevia	
2 tablespoons water	30 ml

In a bowl, combine all spices and stevia. In another bowl, beat egg white with water until frothy. Add pecans to egg mixture and coat well. Place coated pecans on a greased baking sheet and sprinkle spice mixture over nuts. Bake at 300 degrees for 30 minutes. Allow to cool before serving.

Makes four ½ cup servings

PER SERVING: 11G CARBOHYDRATE; 367 CALORIES; 37G TOTAL FAT; 5G PROTEIN •
FOOD EXCHANGES: ½ STARCH; ½ LEAN MEAT; 7 FAT

Roasted Garlic Dip

A special treat for two, or you will be eating alone.

1 garlic bulb	1
½ cup sour cream	120 ml
½ cup mayonnaise	120 ml
1 tablespoon chives, chopped	15 ml
salt & pepper to taste	
¼ teaspoon green stevia powder	1.25 ml

On a grill or in an oven, roast garlic bulb for about 15-20 minutes or until cloves become soft and dry. Peel garlic gloves and mash in a bowl. Add mashed garlic to remaining ingredients and mix well. Refrigerate for at least 2 hours to let flavors blend. Serve with fried cheese, protein crisps or vegetable sticks.

Makes four ¼-cup servings

NUTRITIONAL FACTS PER SERVING: 2G CARBOHYDRATE; 260 CALORIES; 29G TOTAL FAT; 1 G PROTEIN • FOOD EXCHANGES: 3 FAT

Eggplant Dip

An enjoyable treat from the Middle East. Remember to use a high-quality olive oil.

1 large eggplant	1 large
3 tablespoons olive oil	45 ml
salt & pepper to taste	
1 medium tomato	1 medium
¼ cup green onion, chopped	60 ml
½ cup bell pepper, chopped	120 ml
2 tablespoons lemon juice	30 ml
¼ cup black olives	60 ml

Cut eggplant in half lengthwise. Brush 1 tablespoon of olive oil over the surface of the eggplant and place on a grill over medium heat. Grill until eggplant is soft, about 20-30 minutes depending on the eggplant. Remove and allow the eggplant to cool.

Scrape eggplant from the skin and place into a food processor with remaining olive oil. Puree eggplant and add remaining ingredients. Serve with fried cheese or protein crisps. Also wonderful with grilled chicken.

Makes eight ¼-cup servings

NUTRITIONAL FACTS PER SERVING: 6G CARBOHYDRATE; 72 CALORIES; 6G TOTAL FAT; 1G PROTEIN • FOOD EXCHANGES: 1 VEGETABLE; 1 FAT

Black Olive Paté

This dish is a must with the eggplant dip.

1⅓ cups black olives, pitted	315 ml
⅔ cup green olives, pitted	160 ml
¾ cup olive oil	175 ml
1 clove garlic, peeled	1 clove
1 tablespoon lemon juice	15 ml
¼ cup cilantro	60 ml
½ cup yellow onion, chopped	120 ml

Place all ingredients into food processor and puree until smooth. Serve with protein crisps or fried cheese.

NUTRITIONAL FACTS PER RECIPE: 4G CARBOHYDRATE; 405 CALORIES; 44G TOTAL FAT; TRACE PROTEIN • FOOD EXCHANGES: ½ VEGETABLE; 9 FAT

Cheese Rarebit

2 tablespoons butter	30 ml
1 pound sharp cheddar cheese, shredded	455 g
1 cup beer	235 ml
1 egg, beaten	1
1 teaspoon dry mustard	5 ml
1 teaspoon paprika	5 ml
⅛ teaspoon stevioside	½ ml
or 1 teaspoon stevia blend	5 ml
or 2 packets of stevia	

Melt butter in top of double boiler over hot water and add cheese. Stir until cheese begins to melt. Add beer gradually, stirring constantly until cheese is melted and mixture is smooth. Stir in egg, mustard, paprika, and stevia. Serve at once.

Can be served as a type of fondue, dip or even a sauce over eggs.

Makes 4 servings

NUTRITIONAL FACTS PER SERVING: 4G CARBOHYDRATE; 552 CALORIES; 45G TOTAL FAT; 30G PROTEIN • FOOD EXCHANGES: 4 LEAN MEAT; 6½ FAT

Mushroom Stuffing

6 tablespoons butter	90 ml
2 cups leeks, chopped	475 ml
1 cup shallot, chopped	235 ml
2 cups celery, chopped	475 ml
1 ounce porcini mushroom, sliced	30 g
1¼ pounds button mushroom, sliced	570 g
½ pound shiitake mushroom, sliced	225 g
1 cup fresh parsley, chopped	235 ml
1 cup walnut, chopped	235 ml
3 tablespoons fresh thyme, chopped	45 ml
2 tablespoons fresh sage, chopped	30 ml
2 eggs	2
salt and pepper, to taste	

Melt butter in a large skillet and gently sauté leeks, shallot and celery until tender. Remove from heat and allow vegetables to cool. Once cool, mix all remaining ingredients until well incorporated. Use as a stuffing for a turkey, large chicken or for 3–5 Cornish hens. If stuffing a bird is not desired, use a little chicken stock and gently sauté over medium heat until mushrooms are tender.

Makes 16 servings

NUTRITIONAL FACTS PER SERVING: 18G CARBOHYDRATE; 166 CALORIES; 10G TOTAL FAT; 5G PROTEIN • FOOD EXCHANGES: ½ STARCH; ½ LEAN MEAT; 1½ VEGETABLE; 1½ FAT

Wild Rice & Mushroom Stuffing

A wonderful stuffing for the Pesto Roasted Cornish Hens (see Index).

¼ cup wild rice	60 ml
4 cups water	1 liter
1 tablespoon olive oil	15 ml
½ cup onion, minced	120 ml
½ cup celery, chopped	120 ml
1 teaspoon garlic, minced	5 ml
3 cups mushroom, sliced	710 ml
½ pound sausage	225 g
2 tablespoons parsley, minced	30 ml
2 tablespoons cilantro, minced	30 ml

In a small saucepan, combine wild rice with water and salt to taste. Bring to a boil. Cover and reduce heat and simmer until tender, about 45 minutes. In a skillet, sauté onions, celery and garlic until onion is clear. Add mushrooms and sauté until mushrooms are soft. Remove from heat. Cook sausage until done. Drain rice, if necessary, and add to mushroom mixture. Stir in parsley, sausage and cilantro. Serve as a side dish or as stuffing for turkey, chicken or Cornish hens.

Makes 6 servings

NUTRITIONAL FACTS PER SERVING: 9G CARBOHYDRATE; 220 CALORIES; 18G TOTAL FAT; 7G PROTEIN • FOOD EXCHANGES: ½ STARCH; ½ LEAN MEAT; ½ VEGETABLE; 3 FAT

Pickled Eggs

Need a snack? Try a couple of these.

1½ cups apple cider vinegar	360 ml
1 teaspoon pickling spice	5 ml
1 clove garlic, minced	1 clove
1 fresh bay leaf	1
6 hard-boiled eggs, peeled	6
⅛ teaspoon stevioside	½ ml
or 1 teaspoon stevia blend	5 ml
or 2 packets of stevia	

Simmer vinegar and spices uncovered for 10 minutes; cool slightly, add garlic and bay leaf. Pack eggs into a screw-top jar, add vinegar mixture; cover and refrigerate 7-10 days before serving, longer for stronger flavor.

Makes 6 servings

NUTRITIONAL FACTS PER SERVING: 4G CARBOHYDRATE; 88 CALORIES; 5G TOTAL FAT; 6G PROTEIN • FOOD EXCHANGES: 1 LEAN MEAT; ½ FAT

Pickled Vegetables

2 cups zucchini, washed & thinly sliced	475 ml
2 cups yellow squash, washed & thinly sliced	475 ml
½ cup onion, thinly sliced	120 ml
salt	
1½ cups apple cider vinegar	360 ml
1½ teaspoons stevioside	7.5 ml
or 12 teaspoons stevia blend	60 ml
or 24 packets of stevia	
1½ tablespoons pickling spice	23 ml
1 red bell pepper, thinly sliced	1

Lightly coat vegetables with salt. Let stand for about 30 minutes. Rinse vegetables in cold water and drain thoroughly.

In a medium saucepan, combine vinegar, stevia and spices and bring to a boil. Add bell pepper and remove from heat. Allow sauce to cool. Stir in sliced vegetables. Spoon mixture into sterilized jars and cover. Refrigerate for up to 3 weeks or follow canning procedures for longer storage.

Makes 16 servings

NUTRITIONAL FACTS PER SERVING: 4G CARBOHYDRATE; 15 CALORIES; TRACE TOTAL FAT; 1G PROTEIN • FOOD EXCHANGES: ½ VEGETABLE

Sweet Pickles

4 cups cucumber, thinly sliced	950 ml
2 cloves garlic	2 cloves
1¾ cups water	410 ml
1 teaspoon mustard seed	5 ml
1 teaspoon celery seed	5 ml
1 teaspoon ground turmeric	5 ml
1 teaspoon stevioside	5 ml
or 8 teaspoons stevia blend	40 ml
or 16 packets of stevia	
2 cups onion	475 ml
2 cups apple cider vinegar	475 ml

Place cucumbers and garlic in a glass bowl (do not use metal). Set aside. In a saucepan, stir together spices and stevia in water. Bring to a boil. Stir in onions. Boil for about 2 minutes then remove from heat. Stir in vinegar. Pour mixture over cucumber slices. Allow to cool and then place in an airtight container. Refrigerate for at least 24 hours before serving.

Makes sixteen ⅛-cup servings

NUTRITIONAL FACTS PER SERVING: 5G CARBOHYDRATE; 18 CALORIES; TRACE TOTAL FAT; 1G PROTEIN • FOOD EXCHANGES: ½ VEGETABLE

Stuffed Jalapeños

By far, one of my favorite recipes.

16 jalapeños	16
¼ cup sharp Cheddar cheese	60 ml
¼ cup cream cheese	60 ml
2 cups Pancake Mix (see Index)	475 ml
¼ cup beer	60 ml
oil, for frying	

It is wise to wear rubber gloves while preparing this recipe. Wash jalapeños and remove the top of the pepper. With a small paring knife, remove seeds from inside the pepper while being careful not to cut the external wall. Pat peppers dry with a towel and set aside.

In a food processor, blend cheeses together until smooth. Spoon cheese mixture into each pepper.

Prepare pancake mix as per instructions except add additional beer. Pancake mix should be thin but not runny. Heat oil over medium heat. When oil is heated, dip each pepper into pancake mix and coat well. WIth a spoon or fork, lower coated pepper into hot oil. Fry until golden brown. Remove. Serve with your favorite dipping sauce.

Yield: 8 servings of 2 peppers

NUTRITIONAL FACTS PER SERVING: 2G CARBOHYDRATE; 104 CALORIES; 9G TOTAL FAT; 3G PROTEIN • FOOD EXCHANGES: ½ LEAN MEAT; ½ VEGETABLE; 1½ FAT

Note: You can use this recipe to deep fry almost anything ranging from fried fish to fried mushrooms. Simply substitute your favorite vegetable for the Jalapeños.

Sun-Dried Tomato Appetizers

¼ cup sun-dried tomatoes, oil-packed	60 ml
¼ pound mozzarella cheese, diced	115 g
2 tablespoons fresh basil leaves, minced	30 ml
1 garlic clove, minced	1 clove
black pepper, to taste	
1 pint cherry tomatoes	475 ml
¼ cup olive oil	60 ml

Drain sun-dried tomatoes and pat dry. Finely mince the tomatoes. Cut mozzarella into ¼-inch cubes. In a bowl, combine the cheese, basil, garlic, sun-dried tomatoes and black pepper. Add the olive oil and blend well. Cover and refrigerate 1 hour to blend flavors. (Note: you can use the oil from the tomatoes if it is a good quality oil, but only use enough to make ¼ cup total.)

Just before serving, prepare cherry tomatoes by removing the stem end, cutting a thin slice from bottom of tomato to keep it setting straight and removing center from tomatoes with melon baller or small spoon. Sprinkle inside of tomatoes very lightly with salt and invert on paper towels to drain briefly. Stuff the tomatoes with the cheese mixture, garnish with small basil leaves and serve immediately.

Makes 20 servings

NUTRITIONAL FACTS PER SERVING: 1G CARBOHYDRATE; 48 CALORIES; 4G TOTAL FAT; 1G PROTEIN • FOOD EXCHANGES: 1 FAT

Stuffed Mushrooms with Cheese

These stuffed mushrooms remind me of mini-pizzas.

8 ounces mushrooms	230 g
¼ cup Worcestershire Sauce	60 ml
1 egg, beaten	1
4 ounces pepperoni slices	115 g
8 ounces mozzarella cheese, shredded	230 g
½ cup chopped onions	120 ml
⅛ teaspoon stevioside	½ ml
or 1 teaspoon stevia blend	5 ml
or 2 packets of stevia	

Remove stems from mushroom caps. Wash caps in a bath of lemon-water and set aside to dry. In a large bowl, add remaining ingredients and mix together with your hands so that the mixture sticks together. If mixture is too dry, add another beaten egg.

Place mushroom caps in heavy baking pan and fill each cap with a mound of pepperoni mixture. Use leftover mixture to cover mushrooms already stuffed.

Bake mushroom caps in a preheated oven at 350 for about 30 minutes or until cheese is bubbling. Serve immediately.

Makes 4 servings

NUTRITIONAL FACTS PER SERVING: 9G CARBOHYDRATE; 371 CALORIES; 28G TOTAL FAT; 21G PROTEIN • FOOD EXCHANGES: 3 LEAN MEAT; 1 VEGETABLE; 4 FAT

Sesame Shrimp Cakes

6 ounces shrimp, cleaned	175 g
1 teaspoon ginger root, grated	5 ml
1 garlic clove, minced	1 clove
1 egg white	1
3 pinches Chinese Five-Spice Blend (see Index)	3 pinches
salt & black pepper	
⅛ teaspoon stevioside	½ ml
or 1 teaspoon stevia blend	5 ml
or 2 packets of stevia	
3 tablespoons sesame seeds	45 ml
¼ cup green onion, finely chopped	60 ml
peanut oil for frying	
lemon wedges	

Drain shrimp well on paper towels. Using a sharp knife, finely mince shrimp. In a bowl, mix shrimp with ginger and garlic. Lightly whisk egg white with a fork until frothy. Add to shrimp mixture. Stir in Five Spice Powder, salt and pepper, stevia, sesame seeds and green onions; mix well.

In a frying pan, heat ¼ inch of oil over medium heat. Spoon shrimp mix onto pan to make 4 inch wide cakes. Fry until bottom is pink and crispy. Turn cake and finish cooking until entire cake is pink and crispy. Serve with lemon wedges.

Makes 4 servings

NUTRITIONAL FACTS PER SERVING: 7G CARBOHYDRATE; 109 CALORIES; 4G TOTAL FAT; 11G PROTEIN • FOOD EXCHANGES: 1½ LEAN MEAT; 1 VEGETABLE; ½ FAT

Sausage Won Ton Mini-Muffins

1 pound Italian sausage, ground	455 g
1½ cups Monterey jack cheese, shredded	355 ml
1½ cups red bell pepper, minced	355 ml
2 tablespoons black olives, sliced	30 ml
1 cup ranch salad dressing	235 ml
1 package won-ton wrappers	1 package

Brown sausage until very well done and drain thoroughly. Combine with remaining ingredients except won ton wrappers. Grease mini-muffin tins and place won ton wrappers inside, pressing with fingers to form the shape of muffin cups. Brush wrappers lightly with oil, using sesame and vegetable oil combined if desired.

Bake wrappers in preheated 350-degree oven for 5 minutes. Fill the muffin cups with sausage mixture and bake 5-6 minutes longer until cheese is melted.

Makes 12 servings

NUTRITIONAL FACTS PER SERVING: 4G CARBOHYDRATE; 295 CALORIES; 27G TOTAL FAT; 10G PROTEIN • FOOD EXCHANGES: 1 LEAN MEAT; 4 ½ FAT

Salmon Protein Crisp Appetizers

15 ounces canned salmon, flaked	425 g
8 ounces cream cheese, softened	230 g
1 tablespoon Picante Sauce (see Index)	15 ml
2 tablespoons fresh parsley	30 ml
1 teaspoon cilantro	5 ml
¼ teaspoon ground cumin, optional	1.25 ml
8 8-inch Protein Crisps (see Index)	8
olive oil	

Prepare protein crisps as instructed in the recipe except do not cook. Leave dough in a bowl.

Drain salmon and remove any bones. In a small bowl combine salmon, cream cheese, salsa, parsley and cilantro. Add cumin if desired. Set aside.

Roll out enough protein crisp dough to make an 8-inch round tortilla. Spread about 2 tablespoons mixture over each tortilla. Gently roll each tortilla up tightly and wrap individually with plastic wrap. Refrigerate 2-3 hours; Heat oil over medium heat and then sauté each rolled tortilla until crisp. Slice each tortilla into bite-size pieces.

Makes eight tortilla rolls (about 48 bite-size pieces)

NUTRITIONAL FACTS PER SERVING: 7G CARBOHYDRATE; 68 CALORIES; 3G TOTAL FAT; 3G PROTEIN • FOOD EXCHANGES: ½ STARCH; ½ FAT

Porcupine Appetizers

Strange name but very tasty.

1 pound ground beef	455 g
1 tablespoon onions, minced	15 ml
2 tablespoons green bell pepper, finely chopped	30 ml
½ teaspoon salt	2.5 ml
½ teaspoon celery salt	2.5 ml
1 clove garlic, minced	1 clove
2 cups tomato juice	475 ml
¼ teaspoon stevioside	1.25 ml
or 2 teaspoons stevia blend	10 ml
or 4 packets of stevia	
½ teaspoon oregano	2.5 ml
2 tablespoons Worcestershire sauce	30 ml

Combine ground beef, onion, green pepper, salt, celery salt and garlic; form into balls about 1½ inches in diameter.

In a large saucepan, heat tomato juice, garlic cloves, stevioside, oregano and Worcestershire sauce. Simmer over medium heat for about 10 minutes. Add meatballs. Cover tightly and simmer for 50 minutes. Remove garlic cloves before serving.

Makes 6 servings

NUTRITIONAL FACTS PER SERVING: 8G CARBOHYDRATE; 270 CALORIES; 21G TOTAL FAT; 14G PROTEIN • FOOD EXCHANGES: 2 LEAN MEAT; ½ VEGETABLE; 3 FAT

Lemon-Olive Meatball Appetizers

12 bacon slices	12 each
1 pound ground beef	455 g
3 tablespoons lemon juice	90 ml
1 teaspoon salt	5 ml
1 cup Cheddar cheese, grated	235 ml
12 olives, minced	12 each
¼ green bell pepper finely chopped	¼
½ cup milk	120 ml
1 egg, beaten	1

Partially cook bacon but don't allow it to curl. In a large bowl, mix all ingredients except bacon. Shape mixture into 12 balls. Wrap a bacon slice around each ball; fasten with a toothpick. Arrange in baking dish. Bake in preheated 350-degree oven for about 40 minutes, turning once or twice.

Makes 12 meatballs (4 servings)

NUTRITIONAL FACTS PER SERVING: 4G CARBOHYDRATE; 631 CALORIES; 52G TOTAL FAT; 34G PROTEIN • FOOD EXCHANGES: 4½ LEAN MEAT; 7½ FAT

Pecan Breaded Oysters

If you love oysters, you'll love this recipe.

2 vanilla beans, split in half	2
1 medium cucumber, peeled, seeded & diced	1 medium
4 ounces heavy cream	120 ml
4 ounces unsalted butter	115 g
1 pinch salt	1 pinch
1 pinch black pepper	1 pinch
2 large plum tomatoes, peeled, seeded, diced	2 large
5 ounces pecan halves	145 g
16 raw oysters, reserve bottom shell	16 each
1 tablespoon butter, or vegetable oil	15 ml

THE SAUCE

To prepare sauce, combine first three ingredients and bring to a boil. Reduce slightly, allowing vanilla flavor to come out. Whisk in butter. Season to taste. Add tomatoes and set aside.

THE OYSTERS

To prepare oysters, grind pecans in food processor, making "pecan meal." Dredge oysters in pecan meal. Sauté in small nonstick pan with vegetable oil or butter for two minutes on each side over high heat.

Place four shells on each of four plates, spoon sauce into shells, and place one oyster on top of each.

Makes 4 servings

NUTRITIONAL FACTS PER SERVING: 14G CARBOHYDRATE; 608 CALORIES; 61G TOTAL FAT; 7G PROTEIN • FOOD EXCHANGES: ½ STARCH; ½ LEAN MEAT; 1 VEGETABLE; 12 FAT

⑩

Main Dishes

Main Dishes

Protein Pasta

Pasta, especially this recipe, is not the easiest food to make, but it is well worth the trouble.

¼ cup rolled oat flour	60 ml
½ cup wheat gluten	120 ml
1⅓ cups soy protein isolate	315 ml
¾ teaspoon salt	3.7 ml
4 eggs, beaten	4
⅓ cup water	80 ml
2 tablespoons olive oil	30 ml

In a large bowl, mix oat flour, gluten, soy protein and salt. Make a well in the center of the mixture. In another bowl, combine eggs, water and oil. Beat well and then add to well in flour mixture. Oil hands well and knead dough until it develops a smooth texture. Break dough up into balls about the size of baseballs.

Oil the kneading surface with extra olive oil. Flatten one ball and then thinly roll out. Dough will be fragile. Gently, cut into strips or desired shapes. Store fresh pasta in the refrigerator. Cook fresh pasta by immersing in boiling water until tender about 8 minutes.

Makes 12 servings

PER SERVING: 1G CARBOHYDRATE; 82 CALORIES; 4G TOTAL FAT; 10G PROTEIN • FOOD EXCHANGES: 1½ LEAN MEAT; ½ FAT

Lasagna

Sauce

1 pound sweet Italian sausage	455 g
16 ounces canned tomatoes	455 g
12 ounces tomato paste	345 g
1 tablespoon basil	15 ml
1 clove garlic	1 clove
3 teaspoons salt	15 ml
Protein Pasta, cut into lasagna noodles (see Index)	

Cheese Layer

3 cups ricotta cheese	710 ml
½ cup Parmesan cheese or romano cheese	120 ml
2 tablespoons chopped parsley	30 ml
2 egg, beaten	2
2½ teaspoon pepper	2.5 ml
1 pound sliced Mozzarella cheese	455 g

Preheat oven to 375°F. Brown sausage; add tomatoes, tomato paste, basil, garlic, half the measure of salt and simmer 30 minutes. Cook Protein Pasta noodles, drain and hold in cool water until ready. Mix cottage cheese, Parmesan cheese, eggs, parsley, remaining salt and pepper.

Layer lasagna in large greased pan, starting with sauce, cheese mixture, Mozzarella cheese, noodles and then repeat. Finish with cheese prior to baking. Bake 35 at 350 degrees for 35-45 minutes; let rest for 10 minutes before cutting to serve.

Makes 12 servings.

PER SERVING: 8G CARBOHYDRATE; 163 CALORIES; 12G TOTAL FAT; 7G PROTEIN • FOOD EXCHANGES: 1 LEAN MEAT; 1½ VEGETABLE; 2 FAT;

Tomato Quiche

½ cup chopped onions	120 ml
½ cup green bell peppers – chopped	120 ml
2 tablespoons olive oil	30 ml
1 garlic clove – minced	1 clove
2 pounds tomatoes	900 g
½ teaspoon basil	2.5 ml
½ teaspoon oregano	2.5 ml
½ teaspoon salt	2.5 ml
⅛ teaspoon black pepper	½ ml
3 tablespoons chopped fresh parsley	45 g
¼ teaspoon stevioside	1.25 ml
or 2 teaspoons stevia blend	10 ml
or 4 packets of stevia	
4 large eggs	4
3 tablespoons tomato paste	45 g
Pie Crust (see Index)	
12 black olives – sliced	12 each
⅓ cup grated Parmesan cheese	80 ml
8 anchovies – optional	8 each

Sauté onions, green pepper and garlic in 2 tablespoons oil in a heavy skillet. Add tomatoes that have been peeled, chopped and seeded. Add the basil, oregano, salt, black pepper, parsley and stevia. Cover and cook over low heat for 5 minutes. Remove cover and raise heat so liquid evaporates. Do not let mixture scorch. Remove from heat.

Put 1 egg and 3 egg yolks along with tomato paste into a bowl and mix well. Combine with tomato mixture then pour into pie crust. Top with olives, grated cheese and anchovies if you are using them. Bake about 30 minutes or until firm and golden brown. Let cool for about 5-10 minutes to allow the quiche to set. If you want to serve the quiche piping hot, reheat each slice in a microwave.

Makes 6 servings

PER SERVING: 11G CARBOHYDRATE; 177 CALORIES; 11G TOTAL FAT; 9G PROTEIN •
FOOD EXCHANGES: 1 LEAN MEAT; 2 VEGETABLE; 1½ FAT

Crunchy Cheese Tacos

½ pound ground beef	225 g
½ teaspoon cumin	2.5 ml
¼ cup onion, diced	60 ml
1 clove garlic, minced	1 clove
to taste salt and pepper	to taste
1 large tomato	1 large
¼ head lettuce	¼ head
4 cups cheddar cheese, shredded	1 liter
5 tablespoons oil	75 ml
4 tablespoons sour cream	60 ml

In a large frying pan, sauté beef and then drain the fat from the beef. Add cumin, onion, garlic, and salt & pepper and sauté until thoroughly blended. Set aside.

Dice tomatoes into small cubes and place into a bowl. Shred lettuce or slice very thin and place into a separate bowl.

In a large nonstick frying pan, heat up about 1 tablespoon of oil over medium heat. Sprinkle one cup of shredded cheddar cheese over oil to form a 5-inch "pancake". Allow the cheese to melt and bubble until the edges become crisp and the cheese is firm. Using a spatula, carefully turn the cheese over and cook until cheese starts to become crispy. Fold cheese pancake in half and cook both sides until the cheese is very crispy. Remove from heat and place on a paper towel to drain. Repeat process to make 4 cheese taco shells.

Fill each shell with meat, sour cream, lettuce and tomato. Serve immediately.

Makes 4 tacos

PER SERVING: 5G CARBOHYDRATE; 828 CALORIES; 73G TOTAL FAT; 39G PROTEIN • FOOD EXCHANGES: 5½ LEAN MEAT; ½ VEGETABLE; 11 1/2 FAT

Egg Foo-Yung

4 eggs	4
½ teaspoon salt	2.5 ml
1 tablespoon soy sauce	1 ml
⅛ teaspoon stevioside	½ ml
or 1 teaspoon stevia blend	5 ml
or 2 packets of stevia	
2 tablespoons vegetable oil	30 ml
¼ pound pork, diced	115 g
1 stalk celery, diced	1 stalk
1 scallion, cut into 1" pieces	1
½ cup bean sprouts	½ cup

Lightly beat the eggs with ½ teaspoon salt. In a separate bowl, mix the soy sauce and stevia.

In a frying pan, heat oil over medium heat and then stir-fry the pork for about a minute. Add the celery, scallion and bean sprouts and stir for a minute more. Add the soy sauce and stevia and simmer for another minute, then drain the liquid into a bowl or cup. Add the egg mixture, stir to mix the pan contents into it, then let it cook without stirring. Flip the eggs over when the bottom is brown and crisp and continue cooking until both sides are done through. Transfer to a plate. Pour pan juices over eggs and serve hot.

Makes 4 servings

PER SERVING: 5G CARBOHYDRATE; 209 CALORIES; 16G TOTAL FAT; 12G PROTEIN •
FOOD EXCHANGES: 1½ LEAN MEAT; ½ VEGETABLE; 2½ FAT

Avocado Cream Sauce Over Grilled Chicken

This recipe is a favorite for avocado lovers.

4 chicken breast halves	4
olive oil	
salt and pepper	
2 tablespoons lime juice	30 ml
⅛ teaspoon stevioside	½ ml
or 1 teaspoon stevia blend	5 ml
or 2 packets of stevia	
2 avocados	2
1 clove garlic, quartered	1 clove
2 tablespoons chives, chopped	30 ml
1 tablespoon cilantro, chopped	15 ml
½ tablespoon tarragon, chopped	8 ml
2 tablespoons butter	30 ml
¼ cup heavy cream	60 ml

Pat dry chicken breasts. Lightly coat the breasts in olive oil and salt and pepper to taste. Place breasts on a grill over medium heat and cook 8 minutes, turn and cook about another 7-8 minutes or until breasts are done (when the meat is completely white through the breast).

Peel and pit avocados. In a food processor or blender, puree avocados, lime juice, garlic, stevioside and herbs. In a saucepan, melt butter over low heat. Stir in puree and cook over low heat, stirring occasionally. When heated through, add cream and continue to heat but do not boil. Salt to taste. Serve over grilled chicken breasts.

Serves 4

PER SERVING: 9G CARBOHYDRATE; 517 CALORIES; 40G TOTAL FAT; 33G PROTEIN •
FOOD EXCHANGES: 4½ LEAN MEAT; ½ FRUIT; 5½ FAT

Smothered Chicken

4 chicken breast halves, boneless	4
olive oil	
2 tablespoons butter	30 ml
2 cups button mushrooms, sliced	475 ml
1 clove garlic, minced	1 clove
¼ cup dry white wine	60 ml
to taste salt and pepper	to taste
8 slices bacon	8 slices
8 ounces provolone cheese, sliced	230 g

Coat chicken breasts in olive oil and grill over medium heat for about 12-15 minutes or until breasts are done. Take care not to overcook the chicken, because this will dry the meat.

In a saucepan, melt butter and sauté sliced mushrooms and garlic until tender. Add wine and sauté for another 5 minutes. Salt and pepper to taste.

In a frying pan, fry bacon until long and crispy. Remove and drain on paper towels.

Place each chicken breast on a baking pan. Place ¼ of the mushroom mixture over each breast. Place 2 bacon slices over the mushrooms and cover with provolone cheese. Bake at 350°F for 5-10 minutes or until cheese has melted and started to brown. Serve hot.

Makes 4 servings

PER SERVING: 2G CARBOHYDRATE; 393 CALORIES; 25G TOTAL FAT; 35G PROTEIN • FOOD EXCHANGES: 5 LEAN MEAT; ½ VEGETABLE; 2 FAT

Sweet & Sour Chicken

2 pounds chicken, sliced into strips	1,360 g
1 tablespoon soy sauce	15 ml
2 tablespoons butter	30 ml
½ teaspoon ginger	2.5 ml
1 egg white	1
1 each red & green bell peppers, sliced	2
2 tablespoons butter	30 ml
1 cup Sweet & Sour Sauce (see Index)	240 ml

Marinate chicken in soy sauce for about 30 minutes. In a frying pan, melt butter. Gently sauté ginger. Dip chicken strips into egg white and coat well. Sauté chicken in butter until lightly brown. Add pepper strips and sauté for about 3-5 minutes, just until peppers start to get soft. Serve with Sweet and Sour Sauce (see Index).

Makes 4 servings.

PER SERVING: 3G CARBOHYDRATE; 419 CALORIES; 31G TOTAL FAT; 30G PROTEIN •
FOOD EXCHANGES: 4 LEAN MEAT; ½ VEGETABLE; 4 FAT;

Tandoori Chicken

A wonderful aromatic dish

Chicken

1 teaspoon salt	5 ml
½ teaspoon black pepper	2.5 ml
4 chicken breast halves	4
2 tablespoons lemon juice	30 ml

Marinade

1 clove garlic, minced	1 clove
1 tablespoon minced fresh ginger root	15 ml
1 cup sour cream	240 ml
½ teaspoon powdered red pepper	2.5 ml
1 tablespoon curry powder	15 ml
1 teaspoon black pepper	5 ml
⅛ teaspoon stevioside	½ ml
or 1 teaspoon stevia blend	5 ml
or 2 packets of stevia	

Salt and pepper chicken breasts and then place in a bowl. Cover with lemon juice.

In a large bowl, mix the remaining ingredients together. Place chicken breasts into the sour cream sauce and marinate for 8 hours.

Place chicken in a greased baking dish and cover with marinade. Bake covered in a preheated oven at 375°F. for 25 minutes. Then remove cover and continue cooking until done.

Makes 4 servings

PER SERVING: 3G CARBOHYDRATE; 192 CALORIES; 13G TOTAL FAT; 16G PROTEIN • FOOD EXCHANGES: 2 LEAN MEAT; 1 FAT

Chicken Étouffée

1 whole chicken	1 each
1 cup soy protein isolate	235 ml
4 tablespoons cajun seasoning	60 ml
vegetable oil for frying	
1½ cups onion, finely chopped	355 ml
1 cup green bell pepper, finely chopped	235 ml
¾ cup celery, finely chopped	175 ml
6 cups chicken stock	1420 ml
½ teaspoon stevioside	2.5 ml
or 4 teaspoons stevia blend	20 ml
or 8 packets of stevia	

Divide chicken into eight pieces. Sprinkle 2 teaspoons of Cajun Spice on chicken pieces. Combine 2 teaspoons of Cajun spice with soy protein in a plastic bag. Place chicken pieces in the bag and shake to season. Refrigerate for 30 minutes. Repeat seasoning process. In a large skillet, heat about ¼ inch of oil over medium heat. Cook chicken in the hot oil until golden brown. Allow chicken pieces to drain on a paper towel. Combine onion, peppers and celery in a bowl and set aside. In about ½ cup of oil, fry vegetables until slightly soft. Add agar mix and gently sauté until thick.

In a 5-quart saucepan, bring chicken stock to a boil. Add the agar mixture to the stock and stir until dissolved. Add the stevia to the stock and stir until dissolved. Add the chicken to the pot and cook about 5 minutes, stirring occasionally. Reduce heat to low and continue to cook until chicken is tender, about 50 minutes.

Makes 8 servings.

PER SERVING: 8G CARBOHYDRATE; 450 CALORIES; 30G TOTAL FAT; 34G PROTEIN • FOOD EXCHANGES: 4½ LEAN MEAT; ½ VEGETABLE; 3 FAT

Deluxe Buffalo Wings

My all-time favorite dish.

Marinade
½ cup buttermilk	120 ml
3 tablespoons Tabasco sauce	45 ml

Chicken
½ cup soy protein isolate	120 ml
¼ cup pork rinds, crushed	60 ml
1 teaspoon salt	5 ml
1 teaspoon garlic powder	5 ml
1 teaspoon onion powder	5 ml
1 teaspoon cayenne	5 ml
3 pounds chicken wings	1⅓ kg

Sauce
¼ cup ghee* or butter	60 ml
1 tablespoon hot pepper sauce	15 ml
2 tablespoons vinegar	30 ml
¼ cup tomato sauce	60 ml
¼ teaspoon stevioside	1.25 ml
or 2 teaspoons stevia blend	10 ml
or 4 packets of stevia	
¼ teaspoon salt	1.25 ml
½ teaspoon garlic powder	2.5 ml
½ teaspoon onion powder	2.5 ml
¼ teaspoon cilantro	2.5 ml
oil for frying	

Marinade

In a large bowl, mix buttermilk with 3 tablespoons of Tabasco sauce. Marinate chicken wings in buttermilk sauce for 4 hours.

Chicken

In a separate bowl, blend together soy protein, crushed pork rinds and spices. Coat chicken wings in soy mix. Allow to chill in refrigerator for ½ hour. Recoat wings and chill in refrigerator for another ½ hour.

Sauce

Melt ghee or butter in a saucepan. Add spices and sauté for 5 minutes. Set aside. In another saucepan, mix tomato sauce, salt, pepper sauce, stevia and vinegar and let simmer for about 5 minutes. Add this mixture to the ghee mixture and bring to a low boil, stirring constantly until thickened. Remove sauce from the heat and allow to cool slightly.

In a skillet, heat oil and fry chicken until golden brown. Remove chicken and place in a round-bottom bowl. Add sauce and toss chicken until well coated. Serve hot with Ranch or Blue Cheese dressing (see Index).

If you like it spicy, add more pepper sauce, ground jalapeños, or try my favorite, ground habañero peppers.

*Ghee is clarified butter that will not burn at high temperatures. It is available at your local health food store or international market.

Makes 3 servings.

PER SERVING: 7G CARBOHYDRATE; 1384 CALORIES; 130G TOTAL FAT; 47G PROTEIN • FOOD EXCHANGES: 6½ LEAN MEAT; ½ VEGETABLE; 22 FAT

Paprika Roasted Chicken Wings

Use a quality paprika - the difference will amaze you.

3 cloves garlic, minced	3 cloves
¼ cup red wine vinegar	60 ml
¾ cup dry red wine	180 ml
¼ cup water	60 ml
1 teaspoon sweet paprika	5 ml
⅛ teaspoon stevioside	1.25 ml
or 1 teaspoon stevia blend	5 ml
or 2 packets of stevia	
2 teaspoons salt	10 ml
3 pounds chicken wings	1,360 g
Sauce	
⅓ cup mayonnaise	80 ml
1 teaspoon dry sherry	5 ml
¼ teaspoon sweet paprika	1.25 ml
⅛ teaspoon stevioside	½ ml
or 1 teaspoon stevia blend	5 ml
or 2 packets of stevia	

Marinade: In a bowl, combine garlic, vinegar, wine, water, paprika, stevia and salt. Place wings in a largesealable plastic bag. Pour marinade into plastic bag with chicken wings. Seal bag and marinate wings for at least 6 hours.

Preheat oven to 375°F. Place wings in a roasting pan. Pour marinade over wings. Roast wings for 30 minutes. With a fork, turn wings over and roast until marinade is reduced and wings are crisp.

Sauce: Whisk remaining ingredients together in a bowl.

Makes 6 servings as an appetiser.

PER SERVING: 2G CARBOHYDRATE; 386 CALORIES; 30G TOTAL FAT; 23G PROTEIN • FOOD EXCHANGES: 3 LEAN MEAT; 3 FAT

Sweet and Spicy Buffalo Wings

Marinade

3 pounds chicken wings	1,360 g
1 teaspoon salt	5 ml
1 teaspoon garlic powder	5 ml
1 teaspoon onion powder	5 ml
1 teaspoon black pepper	5 ml
1 teaspoon cayenne powder	5 ml

Sauce

¼ cup ghee* or butter	60 ml
½ teaspoon garlic powder	2.5 ml
½ teaspoon onion powder	2.5 ml
¼ teaspoon cilantro	1.25 ml
¼ cup tomato sauce	60 ml
¼ teaspoon salt	1.25 ml
1 tablespoon hot pepper sauce	15 ml
¼ teaspoon stevioside	1.25 ml
or 2 teaspoons stevia Blend	10 ml
or 4 packets of stevia	
⅛ cup vinegar	30 ml
oil, for frying	

Marinade: Coat chicken wings in salt, garlic powder, onion powder, black pepper, and cayenne powder. Chill in refrigerator for ½ hour.

Sauce: Melt ghee in a saucepan. Add spices and sauté for 5 minutes. Set aside. In another saucepan, mix tomato sauce, salt, pepper sauce, stevia and vinegar and let simmer for about 5 minutes. Add this mixture to the ghee mixture and bring to a low boil, stirring constantly until thickened. Remove from heat and allow sauce to cool.

In a pan, heat oil and fry chicken until golden brown. Remove chicken and place in a round-bottom bowl. Add sauce and toss chicken until well coated. Serve hot.

If you like it spicy, add more pepper sauce, ground jalapeños, or try my favorite, ground habañero peppers.

*Ghee is clarified butter that that does not burn at high temperatures. It is available at your local health food store or international market.

Makes three 1-pound servings.

PER SERVING: 5G CARBOHYDRATE; 1364 CALORIES; 130G TOTAL FAT; 46G PROTEIN • FOOD EXCHANGES: 6½ LEAN MEAT; 22 FAT

Pesto Roasted Cornish Hens

These hens are even better when stuffed with Mushroom Stuffing (see Index).

2 Cornish game hens   2
Sweet Pesto Sauce (see Index)

Defrost hens if frozen and clean them well. Rub Sweet Pesto Sauce over the hens and then truse them. (You could stuff them with stuffing if desired, see index for stuffing). Roast hens in oven at 375°F for 20-25 minutes or until done. Baste hens with more pesto sauce every 5-10 minutes during cooking process. Serve hot.

*If you prefer to stuff hens, see Index for stuffings.

Makes 2 servings

PER SERVING: 0G CARBOHYDRATE; 672 CALORIES; 47G TOTAL FAT; 58G PROTEIN • FOOD EXCHANGES: 8 LEAN MEAT; 4½ FAT

Cornish Hens

2 Cornish game hens	2
3 cloves garlic, minced	3 cloves
1 tablespoon thyme	15 ml
2 stalks green onions, chopped	2 stalks
¼ cup Worcestershire sauce	60 ml
½ cup dry white wine	120 ml
1 teaspoon stevia blend	5 ml
or 2 packets of stevia	
⅓ cup dry white wine	80 ml

In a large bowl, place washed and dried hens. In a separate bowl, mix remaining ingredients together to create a marinade. Pour marinade over the hens and allow to marinate for 4 hours in the refrigerator. Remove hens and place in a deep oiled baking dish. Pour marinade over the hens and then cover the baking dish with aluminum foil. Bake in a preheated oven at 350°F for 60-90 minutes or until cooked through. Remove aluminum foil and pour marinade out of the baking dish. Return to oven and continue baking until skin crisps. Serve hens with steamed vegetables.

Makes 4 servings

PER SERVING: 5G CARBOHYDRATE; 377 CALORIES; 24G TOTAL FAT; 30G PROTEIN • FOOD EXCHANGES: 4 LEAN MEAT; 2½ FAT

Fish Fillets with Ginger and Soy

5 pounds fillets mackerel, unskinned	2.25 kg
6 tablespoons rice vinegar	90 ml
¼ teaspoon stevioside	1.25 ml
or 2 teaspoons stevia blend	10 ml
or 4 packets of stevia	
4 cups light soy sauce	950 ml
⅓ cup dark soy sauce	80 ml
¾ teaspoon Chinese five-spice powder (see Index)	3.7 ml
2 tablespoons peanut oil	30 ml
1 tablespoon minced fresh ginger root	15 ml
1 large onion, thinly sliced	1 large
2 cloves garlic, minced	2 cloves
½ tablespoon dark sesame oil	7.5 ml
2 scallions	2 each

Cut fish fillets into 3-inch lengths. In a bowl, mix the rice vinegar with the stevia, soy sauces, and five-spice powder and set aside.

Heat the peanut oil in a large frying pan. Add the ginger, onion, and garlic and cook over medium-low heat until tender. Put the fish pieces, skin side down, in a single layer on top of the vegetables in the pan. Pour the soy mixture over the fish, add enough water just to cover (about 1 cup), and simmer until just cooked through, about 9 minutes. Transfer fish to a large platter and cool.

Bring soy mixture to a boil and cook, stirring occasionally, until reduced to approximately 1½ cups. Remove from heat, strain, and stir in sesame oil.

Remove skin and arrange fish on a serving platter. Pour liquid over the fish, cover, and refrigerate. Recipe can be made to this point several hours ahead.

To serve: Bring fish to room temperature. Slice the scallions into rings and sprinkle over fish.

Makes 12 servings

PER SERVING: 10G CARBOHYDRATE; 285 CALORIES; 7G TOTAL FAT; 44G PROTEIN •
FOOD EXCHANGES: 5½ LEAN MEAT; 2½ VEGETABLE; ½ FAT

Catfish in Cream

A surprisingly delicious dish.

¼ cup olive oil	60 ml
½ medium onion, chopped	1/2
½ bell pepper - sliced	1/2
1½ pounds catfish fillets	680 g
1 tablespoon Cajun Spice (see Index)	15 ml
2 plum tomatoes, diced	2
¼ teaspoon stevioside	1.25 ml
or 2 teaspoons stevia blend	10 ml
or 4 packets of stevia	
½ cup heavy cream	120 ml
2 limes	2
to taste Tabasco sauce, optional	to taste

In a heavy skillet, heat oil and then sauté onion and pepper until onions are clear. Season catfish fillets with Cajun seasoning and then brown in skillet with onions and peppers.

Place catfish fillets in a covered greased baking dish. Cover with onions, peppers, and diced tomatoes. Dissolve stevioside in heavy cream and then pour cream over fish and vegetables. Cover and bake in oven at 375° for 25 minutes. If catfish fillets are very thick, allow 5-10 minutes more to ensure that they are cooked through.

Serve each fillet with cream sauce surrounding each fillet and topped with peppers and tomatoes. Garnish with sliced limes. Try a touch of Tabasco for added spice.

Makes 4 servings.

PER SERVING: 10G CARBOHYDRATE; 416 CALORIES; 30G TOTAL FAT; 30G PROTEIN •
FOOD EXCHANGES: 4 LEAN MEAT; ½ VEGETABLE; 5 FAT

Seafood Medley

A beautiful dinner presentation.

6 ounces sole fillet	175 g
8 whole jumbo shrimp	8 whole
12 large sea scallops	12 large
⅛ teaspoon stevioside	½ ml
or 1 teaspoon stevia blend	5 ml
or 2 packets of stevia	
½ cup white wine	120 ml
2 tablespoons pecans, minced	30 ml
1 tablespoons fresh parsley, chopped	30 ml
2 tablespoons basil, minced	30 ml
1 teaspoon tarragon, minced	5 ml
½ teaspoon salt	2.5 ml
½ teaspoon white pepper	2.5 ml
1 clove garlic, minced	1 clove
2 tablespoons butter	30 ml

Wash all seafood prior to cooking. Cut sole into four slices and place a slice in each of 4 buttered scallop shells. Arrange shrimp and scallops around sole. Dissolve stevia into the wine and then pour the wine over the fish. Sprinkle the top of the seafood with pecans and chopped herbs, and dot with butter. Bake dish in oven at 400°F for 15 minutes or until fish is flaky.

Makes 4 servings.

PER SERVING: 4G CARBOHYDRATE; 165 CALORIES; 7G TOTAL FAT; 17G PROTEIN • FOOD EXCHANGES: 2½ LEAN MEAT; 1 FAT

Shrimp Scampi

3 tablespoons butter	45 ml
3 cloves garlic, minced	3 cloves
1 teaspoon tarragon, minced	5 ml
1 pound shrimp, peeled	455 g
1 each egg, beaten	1 each
1 teaspoon stevia blend	5 ml
or ⅛ teaspoon stevioside	½ ml
or 2 packets of stevia	
¼ cup dry white wine	60 ml
to taste salt & black pepper	to taste
lemon or lime	

Heat a skillet over medium-high heat. Melt butter and sauté garlic and tarragon until garlic is lightly brown. Dip shrimp in egg and place in skillet. Sauté for 2-4 minutes. Dissolve stevioside into white wine and then add with salt and pepper. Sauté for about 3 minutes. Serve with a slice of lemon or lime.

Makes 5 servings

PER SERVING: 2G CARBOHYDRATE; 182 CALORIES; 9G TOTAL FAT; 20G PROTEIN • FOOD EXCHANGES: 2½ LEAN MEAT; 1½ FAT

Cajun Shrimp

1 pound shrimp, peeled	455 g
1 tablespoon lime juice	15 ml
½ teaspoon garlic powder	2.5 ml
½ teaspoon onion powder	2.5 ml
¼ teaspoon thyme	1.25 ml
⅛ teaspoon stevioside	½ ml
or 1 teaspoon stevia blend	5 ml
or 2 packets of stevia	
¼ teaspoon salt	1.25 ml
¼ teaspoon red pepper	1.25 ml
⅛ teaspoon black pepper	½ ml
2 tablespoons olive oil	30 ml
2 teaspoons Tabasco sauce	10 ml
lime wedges	

Peel and wash shrimp. Toss the shrimp with the lime juice in a bowl and coat well. Mix the garlic powder, onion powder, thyme, stevioside, salt, red pepper and black pepper in a small bowl. Sprinkle over the shrimp and toss well.

Coat a large skillet with olive oil. Heat over medium-high heat.

Add the shrimp and cook for 3 minutes, or until the shrimp are pink, stirring constantly. Spoon into a serving dish. Add Tabasco sauce to the skillet and continue to cook until the sauce is reduced by half. Ladle over shrimp. Garnish with lime wedges.

As an appetizer, makes 15 servings.

PER SERVING: 1G CARBOHYDRATE; 49 CALORIES; 2G TOTAL FAT; 6G PROTEIN • FOOD EXCHANGES: 1 LEAN MEAT; ½ FAT

Scallops Newport

4 ounces sea scallops	115 g
2 ounces butter	60 g
⅛ teaspoon stevioside	½ ml
or 1 teaspoon stevia blend	5 ml
or 2 packets of stevia	
¼ cup white wine	60 ml
4 ounces mushrooms	115 g
2 ounces fresh spinach	60 g
2 ounces smoked salmon	60 g

If you purchase fresh or canned scallops, make sure that you wash them well to remove any dirt, shell, etc. In a frying pan, melt butter over medium heat and sauté scallops for about 3 minutes. Dissolve stevia in white wine. Add white wine mixture to pan and continue to sauté for another 3-5 minutes. Add mushrooms, spinach, and smoked salmon and toss. Serve hot. Also makes a nice cold salad.

Makes 2 servings

PER SERVING: 5G CARBOHYDRATE; 326 CALORIES; 72G TOTAL FAT; 17G PROTEIN • FOOD EXCHANGES: 2 LEAN MEAT; ½ VEGETABLE; 4½ FAT

Seafood Gumbo

1 pound shrimp, cleaned	455 g
½ pound crab meat	225 g
1 pound okra, sliced	455 g
¼ cup olive oil	60 ml
1 onion, chopped	1
1 bunch green onions, chopped	1 bunch
½ cup celery, chopped	120 ml
2 sprigs parsley, chopped	2 sprigs
1 bay leaf	1
½ teaspoon thyme	2.5 ml
10½ ounces tomatoes, canned	300 g
1 quarts water	1 liter
to taste salt & pepper	to taste
½ teaspoon stevioside	2.5 ml
or 4 teaspoons stevia blend	20 ml
or 8 packets of stevia	

Clean all seafood prior to cooking. Wash okra and remove stems. Sauté okra in 2 tablespoons olive oil over medium heat for 30 minutes. Stir the okra constantly to prevent burning. In a large soup pot, heat remaining olive oil and sauté onions and celery until soft. Add water, cooked okra, parsley, bay leaf, thyme, tomatoes, stevia and seafood. Salt and pepper to taste. Simmer for 30 minutes. Remove from heat. Refrigerate about 6 hours to allow flavors to blend. Reheat and serve hot.

Makes 8 servings

PER SERVING: 9G CARBOHYDRATE; 187 CALORIES; 8G TOTAL FAT; 19G PROTEIN

Crab Quiche

¼ teaspoon stevioside	1.25 ml
or 2 teaspoons stevia blend	10 ml
or 4 packets of stevia	
½ cup whole milk	235 ml
½ cup mayonnaise	235 ml
2 eggs, beaten	2
1⅔ cups crab meat	315 ml
8 ounces Swiss cheese, sliced & diced	225 g
⅓ cup green onions, sliced	80 ml

Dissolve stevioside into milk. In a bowl, combine milk, mayonnaise and eggs until well mixed. Stir in crabmeat, cheese and green onions. Pour into a well greased 9-inch pie pan. Bake at 350°F for 40 to 45 minutes.

Makes 6 servings.

PER SERVING: 3G CARBOHYDRATE; 347 CALORIES; 29G TOTAL FAT; 21G PROTEIN • FOOD EXCHANGES: 2½ LEAN MEAT; 3 FAT

Chili

An all-meat version that is just plain good eatin!

1 cup onion, diced	235 ml
2 red bell peppers, diced	2
3 tablespoons olive oil	45 ml
2 pounds ground beef	900 g
1 teaspoon cumin	5 ml
1 tablespoon lime juice	15 ml
8 ounces tomato juice	235 ml
2 cloves garlic, minced	2 cloves
2 tablespoons chili powder	30 ml
¼ teaspoon stevioside	1.25 ml
or 2 teaspoons stevia blend	10 ml
or 4 packets of stevia	
2 teaspoons cocoa powder	10 ml
1 teaspoon red pepper flakes, optional	5 ml
1 teaspoon paprika, optional	5 ml
8 ounces Cheddar cheese, shredded	225 g

Sauté onion and bell peppers in a skillet with about 3 tablespoons of oil until onions are clear. Add beef and remaining ingredients except cheese. Sauté until beef is done. Serve hot with shredded cheese as a garnish.

Makes 6 servings.

PER SERVING: 10G CARBOHYDRATE; 722 CALORIES; 60G TOTAL FAT; (74 36G PROTEIN •
FOOD EXCHANGES: 5 LEAN MEAT; 1 VEGETABLE; 9 FAT

Jamaican Beef

1 pound beef brisket	455 g
1 large onion, diced fine	1 large
4 large garlic cloves, minced	4 large
3 chilies, stemmed and minced	3
3 tablespoons vegetable oil	45 ml
1 teaspoons coriander	10 ml
2 teaspoons cumin	10 ml
2 teaspoons turmeric	10 ml
1 teaspoon allspice	5 ml
1 teaspoon cinnamon	5 ml
1 green bell pepper, chopped	1
4 tomatoes, chopped	4
¼ teaspoon stevioside	1.25 ml
or 2 teaspoons stevia blend	10 ml
or 4 packets of stevia	
1 bunch green onions, minced	1 bunch
to taste salt and pepper	to taste

In a crock-pot or large soup pot, place beef with enough water to cover. Cook beef over very low heat for about 4 hours or until meat becomes very tender. Remove beef and with a fork, shred the beef into long thin strands. Place in a bowl and set aside.

In a large skillet, cook the onion, garlic, and chilies in the oil over moderate heat for about 10 minutes, stirring from time to time. Add the beef, herbs, spices, bell pepper, tomatoes and stevia. Cook over high heat for 5 minutes, stirring constantly until the mixture is thick and saucy. Add the green onions and cook for 1 minute. Season the beef with salt and pepper. Serve hot.

Makes 8 servings

PER SERVING: 8G CARBOHYDRATE; 256 CALORIES; 21G TOTAL FAT; 11G PROTEIN •
FOOD EXCHANGES: 1½ LEAN MEAT; 1½ VEGETABLE; 3½ FAT

Stir-Fried Pork with Broccoli

Sauce

4 teaspoons soy sauce	20 ml
1 teaspoon stevioside	5 ml
or 8 teaspoons stevia blend	40 ml
or 16 packets of stevia	
2 teaspoons agar	10 ml
2 teaspoons red wine vinegar	10 ml
2 teaspoons sesame oil	10 ml
2 teaspoons rice wine	10 ml
¼ teaspoon salt	1.25 ml
2 tablespoons fish sauce	30 ml

Pork & Vegetables

2 tablespoons chicken stock	30 ml
1 pound boneless pork tenderloin	455 g
12 ounces broccoli	345 g
1 large red bell pepper, thinly sliced	1 large
4 scallions, thinly sliced	4
1 medium clove garlic	1 clove
1 piece fresh ginger root, 1" long	1 piece
2 tablespoons vegetable oil	60 ml
½ cup cashews, 2 oz.	120 ml
2½ teaspoons agar	12.5 ml

SAUCE

Mix the soy sauce, stevia, vinegar, rice wine, agar, sesame oil, fish sauce, and ¼ teaspoon salt in a small bowl. Set aside.

PORK AND VEGETABLES

For the pork and vegetables, slice the pork thinly against the grain. Cut broccoli into small florets and blanch in a large kettle of boiling water until almost tender, about 3 minutes. Drain well and pat dry. Prepare all remaining vegetables for frying.

In a wok or deep skillet, heat 2 tablespoons oil until hot but not smoking. Stir-fry the red peppers and cashews until pepper starts to get tender. Add the pork. Immediately stir in broccoli, sauce, and chicken stock mixture. Toss until sauce coats ingredients and thickens slightly. Serve immediately.

Makes 4 servings.

PER SERVING: 12G CARBOHYDRATE; 371 CALORIES; 28G TOTAL FAT; 20G PROTEIN • FOOD EXCHANGES: ½ STARCH; 2 LEAN MEAT; 1½ VEGETABLE; 4½ FAT

Chinese Pork Tenderloin

2½ pounds pork tenderloin chops	1125 g
2 tablespoons Hoisin Sauce (see Index)	30 ml
2 tablespoons dry sherry	30 ml
1 tablespoon white wine	15 ml
1 tablespoon soy sauce	15 ml
1 teaspoon Chinese Five-Spice (see Index)	5 ml
½ teaspoon stevioside	2.5 ml
or 4 teaspoons stevia blend	20 ml
or 8 packets of stevia	
1 teaspoon garlic, minced	5 ml

Place tenderloins in a large sealable plastic bag. In a bowl, whisk all remaining ingredients together. Add to pork and seal bag. Shake bag to ensure that pork is well coated. Refrigerate for about 2-6 hours, turning bag every ½ hour.

With a cloth, oil grill with olive oil. Grill tenderloins 10-15 minutes or until done (depending on thickness of the tenderloins).

While tenderloins are cooking, remove marinade from plastic bag and simmer in a small saucepan until thickened. Serve with pork tenderloins.

Makes 4 servings.

PER SERVING: 4G CARBOHYDRATE; 373 CALORIES; 10G TOTAL FAT; 60G PROTEIN • FOOD EXCHANGES: 8½ LEAN MEAT

Lamb Curry

3 tablespoons butter	45 ml
2 medium onions, chopped	2 medium
1 clove garlic, minced	1 clove
1 pound boneless lamb shoulder, cubed	455 g
1½ tablespoons soy protein isolate	22 ml
¾ cup beef broth	175 ml
1 cup sour cream	235 ml
½ teaspoon stevioside	2.5 ml
or 4 teaspoons stevia blend	20 ml
or 8 packets of stevia	
5 teaspoons curry powder (see Index)	25 ml
⅛ teaspoon ground cloves	½ ml
1 seeded ancho chili, chopped	1
salt	

In a heavy skillet, melt butter and sauté onions and garlic until light golden. Remove onions and garlic, leaving as much of the butter as possible. Sauté the lamb cubes, turning constantly until browned. Add the onions and garlic again, the broth, the sour cream and all remaining ingredients. Stirring frequently, simmer for 40 minutes, or until meat is completely tender. Add water or more broth if you desire a thinner sauce. Salt to taste.

Makes 4 servings

PER SERVING: 16G CARBOHYDRATE; 417 CALORIES; 31G TOTAL FAT; 20G PROTEIN • FOOD EXCHANGES: ½ STARCH; 2 LEAN MEAT; 1½ VEGETABLE; 5 FAT

11

Cakes and Cookies

Cakes and Cookies

Raspberry Cheesecake

Crust

2½ ounces almonds	75 g
⅛ teaspoon stevioside	½ ml
or 1 teaspoon stevia blend	5 ml
or 2 packets of stevia	
2 tablespoons soy protein isolate	30 ml
2 tablespoons butter, melted	30 ml

Filling

24 ounces cream cheese	690 g
½ teaspoon raspberry extract	2.5 ml
1 teaspoon stevioside	5 ml
3 eggs	3
10 ounces frozen raspberries, thawed	290 g
1 envelope gelatin	1 envelope
⅛ teaspoon stevioside	½ ml
or 1 teaspoon stevia blend	5 ml
or 2 packets of stevia	
1 cup heavy whipping cream	235 ml

In a food processor, mince the almonds to a fine powder. Add stevia and soy protein. Mix well. In a small bowl, mix the almond powder with melted butter with a fork until crumbly. In a springform pan, spread mix over the bottom of pan. Set aside.

In a large mixing bowl, whip cream cheese, raspberry extract and stevia until fluffy. Add eggs and whip until fluffy.

In a food processor, puree raspberries (save a few for garnish) with gelatin until smooth. Use a sieve to remove seeds. Slowly drizzle the raspberry sauce (reserve ¼ of the sauce for garnish) over the cream cheese mixture and with a knife, swirl the mixture so that it looks "marbleized".

Bake in oven at 350 degrees for 30-45 minutes or until a knife can be inserted and removed clean. Allow to cool for about 1 hour.

In a clean blender, whip up remaining stevia with the heavy whipping cream until firm peaks form. Cover the cheesecake with the whipped cream and remaining raspberry sauce on top with a few raspberries for garnish. Serve cold.

Makes about 12 servings

PER SERVING: 14G CARBOHYDRATE; 528 CALORIES (KCAL); 48G TOTAL FAT; (80% CALORIES FROM FAT); 12G PROTEIN; 201MG CHOLESTEROL; 292MG SODIUM • FOOD EXCHANGES: 0 GRAIN (STARCH); 1 LEAN MEAT; 0 VEGETABLE; ½ FRUIT; 9 FAT; 0 OTHER CARBOHYDRATES

New York Style Cheesecake

24 ounces cream cheese	690 g
1½ teaspoons stevioside	7.5 ml
or 12 teaspoons stevia blend	60 ml
or 24 packets of stevia	
1 envelope gelatin	1 envelope
¼ cup warm water	60 ml
2 egg white	2
2 eggs	2
1 teaspoon vanilla	5 ml
1 cup sour cream	235 ml

In a bowl, beat cream cheese and stevia until fluffy. Dissolve gelatin in warm water. Beat in egg whites, eggs and gelatin. Beat in vanilla and sour cream. Pour mixture over pie crust (see Index). Bake in a preheated oven at 300° F. until firm in center (approximately 45-60 minutes). Remove cheesecake and allow to cool. Refrigerate overnight. Serve with fresh fruit or a sauce if desired.

Makes 12 servings

NUTRITIONAL FACTS PER SERVING: 4G CARBOHYDRATE; 260 CALORIES; 25G TOTAL FAT; 7G PROTEIN • FOOD EXCHANGES: 1 LEAN MEAT; 4½ FAT

Amaretto Cheesecake

Almond Crust

2½ ounces almonds	71 g
⅛ teaspoon stevioside	½ ml
or 1 teaspoon stevia blend	5 ml
or 2 packets of stevia	
2 tablespoons soy protein isolate	30 ml
2 tablespoons butter, melted	30 ml

Filling

24 ounces cream cheese	680 g
1 teaspoon stevioside	5 ml
or 9 teaspoons stevia blend	45 ml
or 18 packets of stevia	
8 ounces heavy cream	227 g
½ teaspoon almond extract	2.5 ml
3 eggs	3

Amaretto Topping (optional)

1 teaspoon gelatin	5 ml
½ cup amaretto Liqueur	118 ml
2 teaspoons almond butter	10 ml
⅛ teaspoon stevioside	½ ml
or 1 teaspoon stevia blend	5 ml
or 2 packets of stevia	

To prepare the crust: In a food processor or blender, mince the almonds to a fine powder. Add stevia and soy protein. Blend well. Place the powder into a small bowl and stir in the melted butter. Spread mix over the bottom of a springform pan. Set aside.

To prepare the filling: In a large mixing bowl, whip soft cream cheese, stevia and heavy cream until light and fluffy. Add almond extract, eggs and whip until fluffy. Pour mix into a springform pan.

Bake in oven at 350 degrees for 30-45 minutes or until a knife can be inserted and removed clean. Allow to cool for about 1 hour. Serve cold.

Optional Topping: Dissolve 1 teaspoon of gelatin into amaretto in a saucepan. Gently heat and slowly add 2 teaspoons of almond butter and stevia. Stir until well incorporated. Pour over top of cheesecake and then refrigerate. Sauce adds 4 carbohydrates per serving.

Makes approximately 12 slices

NUTRITIONAL FACTS PER SERVING: 4G CARBOHYDRATE; 331 CALORIES; 33G TOTAL FAT; 7G PROTEIN • FOOD EXCHANGES: 1 LEAN MEAT; 6 FAT

Londonderry Cheesecake

A wonderful cheesecake for brunch or company!

Crust

1 cup walnuts	240 ml
1 tablespoon wheat gluten	15 ml
½ teaspoon stevioside	2.5 ml
or 4 teaspoons stevia blend	20 ml
or 8 packets of stevia	
¼ cup rolled oat flour	60 ml
1 cup soy protein isolate	240 ml
¼ cup butter	60 ml
1 teaspoon lemon peel, grated	5 ml

Filling

4 8-ounce package cream cheese	900 g
½ cup sharp cheddar cheese, finely shredded	120 ml
1 teaspoon lemon peel	5 ml
½ teaspoon vanilla extract	2.5 ml
2½ teaspoons stevioside	12½ ml
or 20 teaspoons stevia blend	100 ml
or 40 packets of stevia	
½ cup butter or margarine	120 ml
4 egg yolks	4
4 eggs	4
¼ cup beer	60 ml
¼ cup heavy cream	60 ml
½ teaspoon orange zest	2.5 ml

CRUST

In a food processor, process walnuts until finely chopped. Add wheat gluten, stevia, oat flour and soy protein until well mixed. Pour mixture into a large bowl. Cut in ¼ cup butter and 1 teaspoon grated lemon peel. Knead mixture until crumbly and slightly sticky. Press mixture into the bottom and sides of a 9-inch pie pan (springform if you have one but to keep your oven clean, place springform into a large pan to collect any oil that may leak during baking). Bake at 375 degrees for 8-10 minutes until slightly brown and the crust is firm.

FILLING

In a mixer, whip cream cheese until smooth. Add Cheddar cheese and beat until well blended. Beat in lemon peel, vanilla, 2½ teaspoons stevioside (or blend), and remaining ingredients.

Pour batter into cooled pie shell. Bake in a 325 degree oven for 1 hour or until cheese mixture sets (top should be firm to touch). Cool cheesecake in pan on a wire rack. Cake will sink, so don't worry. Loosen cake with a spatula and then remove from pan and place on a plate. Chill and serve cold.

Makes 12 servings

NUTRITIONAL FACTS PER SERVING: 4G CARBOHYDRATE; 514 CALORIES; 50G TOTAL FAT; 13G PROTEIN • FOOD EXCHANGES: 2 LEAN MEAT; 9 FAT

No-Bake Cheesecake

A quick and easy treat.

1 package (envelope) unflavored gelatin	1 package
1 cup boiling water	235 ml
16 ounces cream cheese	455 g
1 teaspoon vanilla	5 ml
⅝ teaspoon stevioside	3 ml
or 5 teaspoons stevia blend	25 ml
or 10 packets of stevia	

In a mixing bowl, dissolve gelatin into the boiling water. Add the cream cheese (previously softened to room temperature) and vanilla and begin to beat until fluffy. Add stevia and continue mixing until very fluffy. Spoon into dessert dishes and refrigerate for about 1 hour until set. Serve cold. Garnish with fruit, your favorite sauce or serve plain.

Makes 4 servings

NUTRITIONAL FACTS PER SERVING: 3G CARBOHYDRATE; 405 CALORIES; 40G TOTAL FAT; 10G PROTEIN • FOOD EXCHANGES: 1½ LEAN MEAT; 7½ FAT

Strawberry Shortcake

A favorite for a warm summer day.

½ **Angel Food Cake** (see Index)	
1 cup strawberries, sliced	240 ml
1 teaspoon lemon juice	5 ml
1 teaspoon Marsala wine	5 ml
1 cup heavy cream	240 ml
1 teaspoon vanilla	5 ml
⅛ teaspoon stevioside	½ ml
or 1 teaspoon stevia blend	5 ml
or 2 packets of stevia	

Prepare angel food cake as directed. Slice cake to make four 4" x 4" squares. Divide these squares into 2 layers.

In a bowl, place sliced strawberries and coat with lemon juice and Marsala wine. Set aside.

In a mixer, whip heavy cream with vanilla and stevioside until firm peaks form.

Place 1 layer of the sponge cake square into a dessert dish or bowl. Spoon a portion of the strawberry mix onto the layer. Add a layer of whipped cream and then add the final layer of cake squares. Top with more strawberries and whipped cream. Serve immediately.

Makes 4 servings

NUTRITIONAL FACTS PER SERVING: 6G CARBOHYDRATE; 285 CALORIES; 23G TOTAL FAT; 15G PROTEIN • FOOD EXCHANGES: 2 LEAN MEAT; 4½ FAT

Angel Food Cake

Delicious when served with Lemon Cream Sauce (see Index).

¾ teaspoon stevioside	3.7 ml
or 6 teaspoons stevia blend	30 ml
or 12 packets of stevia	
⅓ cup rolled oat flour	80 ml
⅓ cup wheat gluten	80 ml
½ cup soy protein isolate	120 ml
12 large egg whites, room temperature	12
1 teaspoon vanilla	5 ml
1½ teaspoons cream of tartar	7.5 ml
2 teaspoons stevioside	10 ml
or 16 teapoons stevia blend	80 ml
or 32 packets of stevia	

Sift ¾ teaspoon stevioside (or blend) together with rolled oat flour, wheat gluten, and soy protein. Set aside. In a large bowl, beat egg whites, vanilla, cream of tartar and 2 teaspoons of stevioside (or blend) till stiff peaks form. Slowly sift about ⅓ cup of flour mixture over stiff egg whites; fold in. Continue sifting and folding remaining flour mixture. Pour batter into greased 10-inch tube pan. Bake at 350 degrees for 30 to 35 minutes or until top springs back from a light touch. Immediately invert cake, but leave in pan. This helps prevent the cake from falling but the cake will not be as big as a sugar/flour-enriched cake. Allow to cool completely. To remove, loosen sides of cake from pan with a knife.

Makes 8 slices

NUTRITIONAL FACTS PER SERVING: 2G CARBOHYDRATE; 68 CALORIES; 1G TOTAL FAT; 13G PROTEIN • FOOD EXCHANGES: 2 LEAN MEAT

Shortbread Cookies

½ cup oat flour	120 ml
1 cup soy protein isolate	235 ml
¼ teaspoon salt	1.25 ml
½ teaspoon stevioside	2.5 ml
or 4 teaspoons stevia blend	20 ml
or 8 packets of stevia	
½ cup butter	120 ml

In a mixing bowl, combine flour, protein, salt and stevia. Cut in butter till mixture resembles fine crumbs and starts to cling. Form the mixture into a ball; knead till smooth. On an ungreased cookie sheet, pat or roll dough into an 8-inch circle. Using your fingers, press to make a scalloped edge. With a knife, cut circle into 16 pie shaped wedges, leaving wedges in the circle shape. Bake in a 325 oven for 25-30 minutes or till bottom just starts to brown and center is set. While warm, cut circle into wedges again. Cool on the cookie sheet for 5 minutes. Remove from cookie sheet; cool on a wire rack.

Makes 16 wedges

NUTRITIONAL FACTS PER SERVING: TRACE CARBOHYDRATE; 51 CALORIES; 6G TOTAL FAT; TRACE PROTEIN • FOOD EXCHANGES: 1 FAT

Pecan Sandies

1 cup butter	235 ml
¾ cup oat flour	175 ml
1½ cups soy protein isolate	355 ml
½ teaspoon stevioside	2.5 ml
or 4 teaspoons stevia blend	20 ml
or 8 packets of stevia	
1 teaspoon vanilla	5 ml
1 cup pecans, finely chopped	235 ml
Topping	
1 cup pecans, finely chopped	235 ml
⅛ teaspoon stevioside	½ ml
or 1 teaspoon stevia blend	5 ml
or 2 packets of stevia	

In a mixing bowl, beat butter with an electric mixer on medium to high speed for 30 seconds. Add about half of the soy protein and oat flour, stevia, vanilla and 1 tablespoon of water. Beat till thoroughly combined. Beat in remaining soy and flour. Stir in 1 cup of finely chopped pecans. In a separate bowl, combine 1 cup finely chopped pecans with stevia. Shape dough into crescents, 1-inch balls or 2-inch fingers. Press into pecan mixture covering the cookies completely. Place on an ungreased cookie sheet. Bake cookies in a 325 degree oven for about 20 minutes or till bottoms are slightly browned. Cool cookies on a wire rack.

Makes 3 dozen

NUTRITIONAL FACTS PER SERVING: 1G CARBOHYDRATE; 86 CALORIES; 9G TOTAL FAT; 1G PROTEIN • FOOD EXCHANGES: 2 FAT

Peanut Butter Cookies

½ teaspoon stevioside	2.5 ml
or 4 teaspoons stevia blend	20 ml
or 8 packets of stevia	
½ cup rolled oat flour	120 ml
1 cup soy protein isolate	235 ml
1 teaspoon baking soda	5 ml
½ teaspoon baking powder	2.5 ml
½ cup butter	120 ml
1 cup natural peanut butter	235 ml
3 eggs	3
½ cup heavy cream	120 ml
1½ teaspoons vanilla	7.5 ml
¾ cup peanuts, chopped	175 ml
2 tablespoons liquid lecithin	30 ml
1 tablespoon glycerin	15 ml

In a small bowl, combine stevia, oat flour, soy protein, baking soda, and baking powder; mix well. In another bowl, combine butter and peanut butter; beat till fluffy. Beat egg, cream, lecithin, glycerin, and vanilla into peanut butter mixture. Slowly add dry ingredients to wet ingredients. Beat till thoroughly combined. Shape dough into 1-inch balls. Place 2 inches apart on an ungreased cookie sheet. Flatten by crisscrossing with the tines of a fork. Top with chopped peanuts. Bake in a 375 degree oven for 7-9 minutes or till bottoms are lightly browned. Cool cookies on a wire rack.

Makes about 36 cookies

NUTRITIONAL FACTS PER SERVING: 1G CARBOHYDRATE; 48 CALORIES; 5G TOTAL FAT; 1G PROTEIN • FOOD EXCHANGES: 1 FAT

Meringue Cookie Treats

Zero carbs – now that's a treat!

2 tablespoons powdered milk	30 ml
⅜ teaspoon stevioside	1.8 ml
or 3 teaspoons stevia blend	15 ml
or 6 packets of stevia	
¼ teaspoon cream of tartar	1.25 ml
¼ teaspoon vanilla	1.25 ml
2 egg whites	2

Mix dry ingredients together. In a separate bowl, beat egg whites. While beating, slowly add the dry ingredients. Beat until mixture is super-stiff. This can take up to 10 minutes. You can not overbeat egg whites. Add vanilla and mix just until blended. Place small, half-teaspoon-size drops on oiled parchment paper. You can use a pastry bag to make the drops. Bake in preheated oven at 350 degrees until dry all of the way through and slightly golden (about 25 minutes). Remove from oven and allow to cool. Store in an airtight container.

Makes about 45

NUTRITIONAL FACTS PER SERVING: TRACE CARBOHYDRATE; 3 CALORIES; TRACE TOTAL FAT; TRACE PROTEIN • FOOD EXCHANGES: 0 EXCHANGES

VARIATION

Chocolate Meringue Cookie Treats: Add 1 tablespoon of cocoa powder when mixing the dry ingredients and then follow remaining instructions. Adds no significant carbohydrates.

Chocolate Almond Butter Cookies

Cookie

½ cup almond butter	120 ml
¾ cup heavy cream	175 ml
2 teaspoons vanilla	10 ml
¼ teaspoon stevioside	1.25 ml
or 2 teaspoons stevia blend	10 ml
or 4 packets of stevia	
2 tablespoons soy flour	30 ml
1 teaspoon baking powder	5 ml

Chocolate Coating

2 tablespoons butter	30 ml
1 ounce unsweetened baking chocolate	30 g
2 tablespoons heavy cream	30 ml
⅜ teaspoon stevioside	1.8 ml
or 3 teaspoons stevia blend	15 ml
or 6 packets of stevia	
½ teaspoon vanilla	2.5 ml

Preheat oven to 350 degrees. In a large bowl, mix all of the cookie ingredients together and blend well. Using a teaspoon, drop cookie dough onto a greased cookie sheet to make about 20 cookies. Bake for about 10 minutes.

In a double boiler, melt butter and chocolate and stir with a wooden spoon. Dissolve stevia and vanilla in heavy cream. While constantly stirring, slowly add the cream to the chocolate in a steady stream. Mix until well incorporated. After cookies have cooled, spread chocolate mixture over each cookie. Allow to cool before serving.

Makes 20 cookies

NUTRITIONAL FACTS PER SERVING: 2G CARBOHYDRATE; 97 CALORIES; 10G TOTAL FAT; 1G PROTEIN • FOOD EXCHANGES: 2 FAT

Refrigerator Peanut Butter Cookies

1 ounce unsweetened baking chocolate	30 g
2 tablespoons butter	30 ml
⅓ cup peanut butter	80 ml
⅓ cup ricotta cheese	80 ml
¾ teaspoon stevioside	3.7 ml
or 6 teaspoons stevia blend	30 ml
or 12 packets of stevia	
1 teaspoon vanilla	5 ml

In a double boiler, melt chocolate and butter. Then stir in peanut butter until well mixed. Stir in remaining ingredients. On wax paper, spoon mixture into 12 balls. Refrigerate until firm.

Makes 12 servings

NUTRITIONAL FACTS PER SERVING: 2G CARBOHYDRATE; 85 CALORIES; 8G TOTAL FAT; 3G PROTEIN • FOOD EXCHANGES: ½ LEAN MEAT; 1½ FAT

Brownies

½ cup butter	120 ml
2 eggs	2
1 ounce unsweetened baking chocolate	30 g
2 tablespoons water	30 ml
2 teaspoons chocolate extract	10 ml
2 tablespoons soy flour	30 ml
½ cup walnuts, chopped	120 ml
½ teaspoon stevioside	2.5 ml
or 4 teaspoons stevia blend	20 ml
or 8 packets of stevia	
3 tablespoons creme de cacao	45 ml

In a mixer, cream butter and then add eggs one at a time. Beat well. In a double boil, melt chocolate with water and chocolate extract. While the butter and eggs are being beaten, stream the melted chocolate into the butter. Add soy flour, walnuts, stevia and creme de cacao and continue mixing until well blended. Add mixture to a greased baking dish and bake at 325° for 15 minutes. Cut into squares. Serve chilled or hot with a scoop of Vanilla Ice Cream (see Index).

Makes 30 servings

NUTRITIONAL FACTS PER SERVING: 1G CARBOHYDRATE; 56 CALORIES; 5G TOTAL FAT; 1G PROTEIN • FOOD EXCHANGES: 1 FAT

Chocolate Gooey Brownies

¾ cup soy protein isolate	175 ml
¾ cup whey protein	175 ml
¾ teaspoon stevioside	3.7 ml
or 6 teaspoons stevia blend	30 ml
or 12 packets of stevia	
¼ cup glycerin	60 ml
¾ cup water	175 ml
3 tablespoons Dutch-process cocoa powder	45 ml
3 tablespoons coconut oil	45 ml

Combine soy, whey and stevia in a food processor. Add remaining ingredients. Pulse on high until a soft dough forms. Remove dough and knead by hand for twenty strokes. Press into an 8 x 5-inch pan and bake at 350°F for 8-10 minutes. Remove from pan and cut into bars while still hot. Allow to cool and store in the refrigerator in an airtight container.

Makes 6 large bars

NUTRITIONAL FACTS PER SERVING: 2G CARBOHYDRATE; 272 CALORIES; 7G TOTAL FAT; 52G PROTEIN • FOOD EXCHANGES: 1½ FAT

Raspberry Silk Bars

With a smooth melt-in-your-mouth texture

1½ cups soy protein isolate	355 ml
3 tablespoons whey protein	45 ml
1½ tablespoons lecithin	22.5 ml
1½ tablespoons glycerin	22.5 ml
¾ cup heavy cream	175 ml
3 tablespoons coconut oil	45 ml
1½ teaspoons stevioside	7.5 ml
or 12 teaspoons stevia blend	60 ml
or 24 packets of stevia	
1½ teaspoons raspberry extract	7.5 ml

Combine soy, whey and stevia in a food processor. Add remaining ingredients. Pulse on high until a soft dough forms. Remove dough and knead by hand for twenty strokes. Press into an 8 x 5-inch pan and bake at 350°F for 10 minutes. Remove from pan and cut into bars while still hot. Allow to cool and store in an airtight container.

Makes 6 bars

NUTRITIONAL FACTS PER SERVING: 1G CARBOHYDRATE; 417 CALORIES; 21G TOTAL FAT; 60G PROTEIN • FOOD EXCHANGES: 4 FAT

12

Delicious Desserts
& Perfect Pies

Delicious Desserts & Perfect Pies

Fried Strawberries

A wonderful surprise for your guests.

Peach Sauce	
1 peach	1
½ tablespoon dark rum	7.5 ml
⅛ teaspoon stevioside	½ ml
or ½ teaspoon stevia blend	2.5 ml
or 1 packets of stevia	

Fried Strawberries	
16 large strawberries	16 large
1 quart oil, for frying	1 liter
1 recipe pancakes (see Index)	1 recipe
¼ cup seltzer water	60 ml
⅛ teaspoon stevioside	½ ml
or ½ teaspoon stevia blend	2.5 ml
or 1 packets of stevia	

PEACH SAUCE

Peel and pit peach. In a food processor or blender, puree peach with rum and stevioside. Set aside.

STRAWBERRIES

Remove stems and wash each strawberry. Gently dry with a towel. Heat oil in a deep fryer. The temperature of the oil should not exceed 375 degrees. Prepare pancake mix as per instruction except add an additional ¼ cup of seltzer water and stevia. (You can substitute beer for seltzer water for a different flavor and to make the batter crispier.) Dip each strawberry into pancake batter and then place into the oil. Cook until golden brown on all sides. Remove from oil and allow the strawberries to dry on a paper towel. Serve with peach sauce either as a dip or drizzle over fried strawberries.

Makes 4 servings

NUTRITIONAL FACTS PER SERVING: 12G CARBOHYDRATE; 258 CALORIES; 13G TOTAL FAT; 25G PROTEIN • FOOD EXCHANGES: ½ LEAN MEAT; ½ FRUIT; 2 FAT

This batter is very good for frying just about anything from Jalapeños to fish. If you don't like your batter sweet, leave out the stevioside.

Fruity Gelatin

A delicious zero-carb treat

1 cup boiling water	235 ml
1 quart seltzer water, cold	1 liter
⅛ teaspoon stevioside	½ ml
or 1 teaspoon stevia blend	5 ml
or 2 packets of stevia	
½ package unsweetened Kool-Aid	½ package
2 envelopes unflavored gelatin	2 envelopes

Dissolve stevia, gelatin and Kool-Aid into 1 cup of boiling water. Once they are well dissolved, allow to cool to room temperature. Pour into a bowl and add cold seltzer water and gently stir until well mixed. Refrigerate until jello sets up and is firm.

Note: This is a wonderful treat that has as many variations as the imagination can think up. Add whipped cream, fresh fruit, etc. Have fun!

Makes 8 servings

NUTRITIONAL FACTS PER SERVING: 6 CALORIES; 0G TOTAL FAT; 1G PROTEIN • FOOD EXCHANGES: 0 EXCHANGES

Three Berry Tart

Not only delicious, but beautiful too!

Crust

½ cup almonds	120 ml
½ cup walnuts	120 ml
1 cup soy protein isolate	235 ml
½ teaspoon stevioside	2.5 ml
or 4 teaspoons stevia blend	20 ml
or 8 packets of stevia	
8 tablespoons butter	120 ml

Filling

1 envelope gelatin	1 envelope
⅓ cup milk	80 ml
1 cup muenster cheese, shredded	235 ml
1 cup yogurt	235 ml
1½ cups sour cream	355 ml
½ teaspoon stevioside	2.5 ml
or 4 teaspoons stevia blend	20 ml
or 8 packets of stevia	
1 tablespoon vanilla extract	15 ml
1 teaspoon lemon zest	5 ml
2 cups strawberries, halved	475 ml
1½ cups blackberries	355 ml
1½ cups blueberries	355 ml
1 cup kiwi fruit, peeled and sliced	235 ml
½ cup raspberries	120 ml
⅛ teaspoon stevioside	½ ml
or 1 teaspoon stevia blend	5 ml
or 2 packets of stevia	
½ teaspoon gelatin	2.5 ml
5 tablespoons water	75 ml

CRUST

In a food processor, crush almonds and walnuts to powder and no large pieces remain. Add soy protein powder and ½ teaspoon stevioside; blend until thoroughly mixed. In a separate bowl, melt butter and add soy mixture. Mix until mixture is well incorporated and crumbly. Press onto the bottom and along sides of a well-greased 12-inch tart pan with a removable bottom. Bake crust at 350 degrees for about 15 minutes or until golden brown.

Filling

In a small saucepan, dissolve gelatin into warm milk. Slowly stir in cheese and cook over medium heat until slightly thickened. Remove from heat and allow to cool. In a separate bowl, beat yogurt, sour cream, ½ teaspoon stevioside, vanilla and lemon zest. With the mixer running, add cheese mixture and beat until smooth. Pour into cooled tart shell and refrigerate for 30 minutes.

Arrange berries and kiwi on top of filling. In a blender, puree raspberries with ⅛ teaspoon stevioside until smooth. Strain to remove seeds. In a saucepan, heat up raspberry mixture, add ½ teaspoon gelatin and enough water to form a light glaze. Stir until gelatin is dissolved. Gently brush glaze over fruit. Refrigerate tart for at least 1 hour.

Makes 16 servings

NUTRITIONAL FACTS PER SERVING: 11G CARBOHYDRATE; 217 CALORIES; 18G TOTAL FAT; 5G PROTEIN • FOOD EXCHANGES: ½ LEAN MEAT; ½ FRUIT; 3 FAT

Raspberry Tiramisu

An elegant treat!

Cake
½ **Angel Food Cake** (see Index)	½

Cream Mixture
⅜ teaspoon stevioside	1.85 ml
or 3 teaspoons stevia blend	15 ml
or 6 packets of stevia	
2 egg yolks	2
2 ounces cream cheese	57 g
5 tablespoons ricotta cheese	75 ml
3 teaspoons marsala wine	15 ml

Delicious Desserts & Perfect Pies

1 cup heavy cream	240 ml
⅛ teaspoon stevioside	½ ml
or 1 teaspoon stevia blend	5 ml
or 2 packets of stevia	
Coffee/Raspberry Sauce	
1 teaspoon vanilla	5 ml
2 cups coffee	475 ml
¼ cup raspberries	60 ml
3 tablespoons cocoa powder	45 ml
⅛ teaspoon stevioside	½ ml
or 1 teaspoon stevia blend	5 ml
or 2 packets of stevia	
⅛ teaspoon stevioside	½ ml
or 1 teaspoon stevia blend	5 ml
or 2 packets of stevia	
mint leaves, for garnish	

This recipe is divided into three layers: cake, cream, and coffee/raspberry sauce. To prepare the cake, follow the instructions for the Angel Food Cake. Once the cake is baked and cooled, slice it thinly and then cut the slices into small cubes. Set aside.

CREAM MIXTURE

In a food processor, puree ⅜ teaspoon stevioside and egg yolks on high speed until pale yellow and thick. Add soft cream cheese and whip until smooth. Add ricotta and Marsala. Mix until incorporated. In a separate bowl, whip heavy cream with ⅛ teaspoon stevioside until firm peaks are formed and then fold in ricotta mixture (save about 8 tablespoons for garnish). Refrigerate.

COFFEE/RASPBERRY SAUCE

First make up 2 cups of very strong coffee and then allow to cool. Add ⅛ teaspoon of stevioside and vanilla to coffee. Soak angel food cake squares in coffee mixture for 10 minutes. Remove cake and place in a bowl. Puree raspberries with remaining coffee, cocoa and ⅛ teaspoon stevioside in a clean food processor or blender.

In dessert glasses (I prefer tall wineglasses for a prettier presentation) place a small amount of the soaked angel food cake. Layer the cream layer over that and then place a layer of coffee/raspberry sauce. Repeat until ingredients are used. Garnish with a tablespoon of whipped cream, mint leaf and 1 raspberry. Serve chilled.

Makes 8 servings

NUTRITIONAL FACTS PER SERVING: 4G CARBOHYDRATE; 200 CALORIES; 16G TOTAL FAT; 10G PROTEIN • FOOD EXCHANGES: 1 LEAN MEAT; 3 FAT

Almond Crème Squares

1 envelope gelatin	1 envelope
1 cup water	235 ml
1¾ cups milk	410 ml
½ teaspoon stevioside	2.5 ml
or 4 teaspoons stevia blend	20 ml
or 8 packets of stevia	
1 teaspoon almond extract	5 ml
¼ teaspoon vanilla	1.25 ml
1 11-ounce can mandarin oranges (optional)	310 g

Dissolve gelatin in water for 5 minutes to soften, then bring to a boil and stir to dissolve. Add the milk and stevia and simmer for 10 to 15 minutes, stirring often. Add the almond extract and vanilla. Pour into an 8 x 8" pan and chill thoroughly in the refrigerator. Cut into squares and serve with the mandarin oranges.

Makes 8 servings

NUTRITIONAL FACTS PER SERVING: 3G CARBOHYDRATE; 34 CALORIES; 2G TOTAL FAT; 2G PROTEIN • FOOD EXCHANGES: ½ FAT

Berry Dreams

A perfect ending to the perfect meal.

2 cups strawberries	475 ml
2 tablespoon lemon juice	15 ml
12 ounces blackberries	340 g
½ teaspoon stevioside	2.5 ml
or 4 teaspoons stevia blend	20 ml
or 8 packets of stevia	
1 cup blueberries	235 ml
1 cup ricotta cheese	235 ml
1 teaspoon vanilla	5 ml
¼ teaspoon almond extract	1.25 ml
mint sprig for garnish	

Wash all fruit and allow to dry. Slice strawberries into thin slices and then lightly coat with 1 tablespoon of lemon juice. Process blackberries (reserve a few for garnish), ⅜ teaspoon stevioside and 1 tablespoon of lemon juice in a food processor until smooth. Strain the blackberry sauce through a sieve to remove seeds. In 8 dessert bowls, spoon blackberry sauce into each bowl evenly. Arrange sliced strawberries, whole blackberries and blueberries on top of the sauce.

In a clean food processor, place ricotta cheese, ⅛ tsp. stevioside, vanilla and almond extract and process until very smooth. Spoon mixture into pastry bag and pipe onto berries. Garnish with mint sprigs to add a little green to the color.

Makes 8 servings

NUTRITIONAL FACTS PER SERVING: 12G CARBOHYDRATE; 99 CALORIES; 4G TOTAL FAT; 4G PROTEIN • FOOD EXCHANGES: ½ LEAN MEAT; ½ FRUIT; ½ FAT

Orange Dreams

½ tablespoon gelatin	7.5 ml
2 tablespoons lemon juice	30 ml
½ cup orange juice	120 ml
¾ teaspoon stevioside	3.7 ml
or 6 teaspoons stevia blend	30 ml
or 12 packets of stevia	
3 tablespoons grated orange zest	45 ml
4 egg whites, whipped to stiff peaks	4
1 cup whipping cream, whipped to stiff peaks	235 ml
½ cup frozen raspberries	120 ml
⅛ teaspoon stevioside	½ ml
or 1 teaspoon stevia blend	5 ml
or 2 packets of stevia	
½ teaspoon vanilla	2.5 ml

Dissolve gelatin in 2 tablespoons cold water. Warm lemon juice, orange juice, and stevia over low heat until stevia dissolves, about 1 minute. Stir in dissolved gelatin and orange zest. Transfer mixture to a bowl set inside a larger bowl filled with ice. Stir occasionally until mixture cools and thickens slightly.

Fold the whipped egg whites into the orange mixture, then fold in the whipped cream. Pour this mixture into six 8-ounce custard cups. Chill until set, about 3 hours.

In a food processor, puree raspberries with stevia and vanilla until smooth. Strain through a sieve to remove seeds.

Unmold Orange Dreams onto chilled plates. Drizzle raspberry purée around each dessert; serve immediately.

Makes 6 servings

NUTRITIONAL FACTS PER SERVING: 10G CARBOHYDRATE; 184 CALORIES; 15G TOTAL FAT; 4G PROTEIN • FOOD EXCHANGES: ½ LEAN MEAT; ½ FRUIT; 3 FAT

Chocolate Cream Cheese Mousse

2 cups heavy whipping cream	½ liter
¾ teaspoon stevioside	8 ml
or 6 teaspoons stevia blend	30 ml
or 12 packets of stevia	
8 ounces cream cheese	225 g
1 teaspoon chocolate extract	5 ml
½ teaspoon vanilla extract	2.5 ml
2 tablespoons cocoa powder	30 ml
1 teaspoon gelatin powder	5 ml
1 tablespoon cold water	15 ml
1 tablespoon hot water	15 ml

In a mixer, whip cream with ¼ teaspoon stevioside until firm peaks form. Place whipped cream in a large bowl and refrigerate until needed.

In a clean mixer, add softened cream cheese and mix until smooth. Add chocolate extract, vanilla extract, remaining stevia and cocoa powder and whip until smooth.

In a glass, dissolve gelatin into cold water and let stand for 5 minutes. Add hot water and stir to dissolve gelatin. Add to mixer and blend until very smooth.

Fold whipped cream into chocolate mixture.

Pour into 8 dessert cups and top with whipped cream and sifted cocoa or layer mousse and whipped cream in a dessert cup.

Makes 8 servings

NUTRITIONAL FACTS PER SERVING: 3G CARBOHYDRATE; 260 CALORIES; 27G TOTAL FAT; 3G PROTEIN • FOOD EXCHANGES: ½ LEAN MEAT; 5 FAT

Mango Mousse

When the mangos are in season, do not pass up this dessert.

1 mango, peeled, sliced & pitted	1
1 envelope gelatin	1 envelope
1 teaspoon mango extract	5 ml
¼ cup cold water	60 ml
3 egg yolks	3
¼ teaspoon stevioside	1.25 ml
or 2 teaspoons stevia blend	10 ml
or 4 packets of stevia	
1 tablespoon lemon juice	15 ml
1 dash salt	1 dash
2 tablespoons rum, optional	30 ml
1 cup heavy cream	235 ml
⅛ teaspoon stevioside	½ ml
or 1 teaspoons stevia blend	5 ml
or 2 packets of stevia	

Process enough mangos to make 1 cup of mango puree. Sprinkle gelatin over cold water in a small bowl. Let stand 1 minute. Beat egg yolks in a saucepan. Whisk in stevia, lemon juice and salt. Cook over medium heat, stirring constantly, until mixture has thickened. Add gelatin and stir until dissolved. Stir in mango puree and rum. Refrigerate until mixture is thick.

Whip heavy cream with ⅛ teaspoon stevioside and fold ½ cup into mango mixture. Refrigerate 4 hours. Garnish with remaining whipped cream and a slice of mango.

Makes 4 servings

NUTRITIONAL FACTS PER SERVING: 11G CARBOHYDRATE; 306 CALORIES; 26G TOTAL FAT; 5G PROTEIN • FOOD EXCHANGES: ½LEAN MEAT; ½ FRUIT; 5 FAT

Crème Brûlée

This dessert is a French favorite.

¾ cup milk	175 ml
2¼ cups heavy cream	535 ml
2 vanilla beans, cut lengthwise	2
½ teaspoon stevioside	2.5 ml
or 4 teaspoons stevia blend	20 ml
or 8 packets of stevia	
1 pinch salt	1 pinch
10 egg yolks	10

Preheat oven to 300°F.

Combine cream, milk, vanilla bean, stevia and salt in a saucepan. Gently heat until the mixture begins to boil. Remove from heat; remove vanilla bean and scrape the seeds into the cream mixture. Let mixture cool to room temperature.

In a separate bowl, beat eggs. While whisking egg yolks, slowly add cream mixture in a steady stream.

In 6 small flan or miniature quiche dishes (about 5 x 1 inches), pour Crème Brûlée mixture until the dishes are 3/4 full. Place dishes in a pan of water that comes halfway up sides of Crème Brûlée dishes. Bake 1 hour at 350° or until the cream is set. Remove the dishes from the hot water bath and set aside to cool.

Makes 6 servings

NUTRITIONAL FACTS PER SERVING: 5G CARBOHYDRATE; 427 CALORIES; 43G TOTAL FAT; 7G PROTEIN • FOOD EXCHANGES: ½ LEAN MEAT; 8 FAT

Crème a la Crème

This rich dessert should be made the day before.

½ teaspoon stevioside	2.5 ml
or 4 teaspoons stevia blend	20 ml
or 8 packets of stevia	
1 envelope gelatin	1 envelope
2 cup heavy cream	475 ml
2 cup sour cream	475 ml
1 teaspoon vanilla	5 ml

In a heavy saucepan, mix together stevia, gelatin and cream until smooth. Let stand for 5 minutes to allow gelatin to soften. Bring to a simmer over low heat and whisk until gelatin dissolves. Transfer to a large bowl and allow to cool. Whisk sour cream and vanilla into the cream mixture until smooth. Pour into a lightly oiled ring mold. Cover with plastic wrap and refrigerate over night.

To serve, dip bottom of mold into hot water for just a moment. Place a serving plate over mold and invert. Carefully remove from mold. Slice and serve.

Makes 8 servings.

NUTRITIONAL FACTS PER SERVING: 4G CARBOHYDRATE; 333 CALORIES; 34G TOTAL FAT; 4G PROTEIN • FOOD EXCHANGES: ½ LEAN MEAT; 7 FAT

Vanilla Pudding

1½ tablespoons cornstarch	22.5 ml
2 cups milk, cold	475 ml
2 eggs	2
⅜ teaspoon stevioside	1.8 ml
⅛ teaspoon salt	.5 ml
1 tablespoon vanilla	15 ml

Delicious Desserts & Perfect Pies

In a saucepan, with the stove off, whisk cornstarch, cold milk, salt and stevioside together. Next, turn on medium heat and continue to stir until mixture thickens and just begins to boil. Remove from heat and stir in vanilla. Pour into pudding cups. Chill until thickened.

Makes 4 servings

NUTRITIONAL FACTS PER SERVING: 10G CARBOHYDRATE; 129 CALORIES; 6G TOTAL FAT; 7G PROTEIN • FOOD EXCHANGES: ½ LEAN MEAT; 1 FAT

VARIATION

Chocolate Pudding: Prepare as above, except add ⅓ cup of Dutch process unsweetened cocoa powder with the stevia.

Flan

2 cups whole milk	475 ml
2 cups heavy cream	475 ml
1 teaspoon stevioside	5 ml
or 8 teaspoons stevia blend	40 ml
or 16 packets of stevia	
5 eggs	5
2 teaspoons vanilla	10 ml

In a heavy saucepan, heat milk and cream to simmering. Stir in stevia until dissolved. In a large bowl, beat eggs until foamy. Gradually whisk hot milk into eggs. Stir in vanilla. Pour milk mixture through a strainer into an ungreased 1-quart casserole or souffle dish; cover with a lid or aluminum foil. Place dish in a roasting pan on middle rack of oven. Pour 2 inches of water into the roasting pan. Bake at 325 degrees until custard is set and a sharp knife inserted near the center comes out clean (1 to 1¼ hours). Remove dish from roasting pan and cool to room temperature on a wire rack. Refrigerate until chilled (5 to 6 hours). Spoon custard into dessert dishes and serve.

Makes 5 servings

NUTRITIONAL FACTS PER SERVING: 8G CARBOHYDRATE; 459 CALORIES; 43G TOTAL FAT; 11G PROTEIN • FOOD EXCHANGES: 1 LEAN MEAT; 8 FAT

Custard

2 eggs	2
1 cup whole milk	235 ml
1 cup heavy cream	235 ml
⅜ teaspoon stevioside	1.8 ml
or 3 teaspoons stevia blend	15 ml
or 6 packets of stevia	
½ teaspoon ground nutmeg	2.5 ml
⅛ teaspoon salt	½ ml
¼ teaspoon vanilla extract	1.25 ml

Preheat oven to 350 degrees. In a food processor combine all ingredients in the bowl and process until well mixed, about 10 seconds. Pour custard into 4 custard cups. Place cups in a baking dish, pour boiling water into the dish to a depth of ½ inch. Bake 1 hour or until a knife inserted in center comes out clean. Serve warm or cold with your favorite sauce or topping.

Makes 4 servings

NUTRITIONAL FACTS PER SERVING: 5G CARBOHYDRATE; 278 CALORIES; 26G TOTAL FAT; 6G PROTEIN • FOOD EXCHANGES: ½ LEAN MEAT; 5 FAT

Pie Crust

This recipe is critical to most of the cheesecake and pie recipes.

2½ ounces almonds	70 g
¼ cup soy protein isolate	60 ml
⅛ teaspoon stevioside	½ ml
or 1 teaspoon stevia blend	5 ml
or 2 packets of stevia	
2 tablespoons butter	30 ml

Delicious Desserts & Perfect Pies

In a food processor, mince the almonds to a fine powder. Add soy protein and stevia. Mix well. In a small bowl, mix the powder with melted butter. Mix with a fork until crumbly. In pie pan, press almond mix into the bottom and upsides of the pan. Bake at 350 degrees for about 8-10 minutes or until golden and crispy.

Makes 1 pie shell

NUTRITIONAL FACTS FOR 1 PIE SHELL: 14G CARBOHYDRATE; 621 CALORIES; 60G TOTAL FAT; 14G PROTEIN • FOOD EXCHANGES: 1 STARCH; 1½ LEAN MEAT; 11 FAT

Lemon Pie

1 envelope gelatin	1 envelope
¼ cup lemon juice	60 ml
16 ounces cream cheese, softened	455 g
¾ teaspoon stevioside	3.7 ml
or 6 teaspoons stevia blend	30 ml
or 12 packets of stevia	
8 ounces sour cream	225 g
¼ cup lemon juice	60 ml
½ teaspoon lemon peel	2.5 ml
1 cup heavy cream, whipped	240 ml
1 baked pie shell	1
¼ cup blackberry sauce (see Index)	60 ml

Sprinkle gelatin over lemon juice in a small saucepan. Let stand 5 minutes to soften. Stir on low heat until gelatin is dissolved.

Combine softened cream cheese and stevia in a mixer. Blend in sour cream, lemon juice and lemon peel. Stir in gelatin. Refrigerate until mixture is slightly thickened but not yet set. Fold in whipped cream. Spoon into crust and refrigerate several hours. Serve blackberry sauce as a garnish.

Makes 8 servings

NUTRITIONAL FACTS PER SERVING: 7G CARBOHYDRATE; 375 CALORIES; 37G TOTAL FAT; 6G PROTEIN • FOOD EXCHANGES: ½ LEAN MEAT; 7 FAT

Strawberry Rhubarb Cream Pie

Piecrust

1 cup Baking Mix (see Index)	237 ml
½ cup pecan flour (ground pecans)	118 ml
4 teaspoons stevia blend	20 ml
½ cup butter (room temperature)	118 ml

Filling

1 cup rhubarb, sliced and frozen	237 ml
1 cup strawberries, sliced frozen	237 ml
5 teaspoons Stevia Blend	25 ml
1 package unflavored gelatin	1 ml
¼ teaspoon strawberry extract (LorAnn®)	1.25 ml
½ teaspoon Madagascar Bourbon Vanilla	2.5 ml
8 ounces cream cheese (room temperature)	.5 kg
5 teaspoons Stevia Blend	25 ml
1 cup heavy whipping cream	237 ml

Preheat oven to 350°F.

CRUST

In a bowl, knead all crust ingredients until a firm dough is made. Divide dough into two balls. Place each ball between two sheets of wax paper. Roll each out to make two-pie shells to fit a 9" pie pan. (Set aside one crust for later.) Remove one layer of wax paper and place (paper side up) into pie pan. Then remove remaining top wax paper. Use your fingers to smooth any broken areas of the piecrust. Prick the bottom of the crust with a fork and bake in a preheated oven at 350° degrees for 10 minutes. Allow crust to completely cool.

FILLING

In a saucepan over medium-high heat, add frozen rhubarb and water. Simmer until tender. Add strawberries and simmer until just heated. Remove mixture from heat. Strain mixture (reserving the liquid). Set aside strawberries and rhubarb. In a bowl, combine 1 cup of the reserved liquid (if necessary add water to make 1 cup) with 1 packet of unflavored gelatin and 5 teaspoons of stevia blend. Stir over medium heat until completely dissolved. In a saucepan, combine the gelatin mixture with the strawberries and rhubarb. Add strawberry and vanilla extract. Allow mixture to cool to touch—do not let mixture gelatinize.

In a mixer, whip cream cheese and 5 teaspoons of stevia blend until fluffy. Add heavy cream and whip until firm peaks form. Fold in the rhubarb / strawberry mixture. Pour mixture into cool piecrust. Place in refrigerator and allow to chill. Garnish with sliced strawberries.

Makes 8 servings

NUTRITIONAL FACTS PER SERVING; 27G CARBOHYDRATE, 455 CALORIES; 35 G TOTAL FAT; 12G PROTEIN

Pumpkin Cream Pie

A wonderful holiday treat.

8 ounces cream cheese	225 g
1 cup canned pumpkin	235 ml
1 cup heavy cream	235 ml
¾ teaspoon stevioside	3.7 ml
or 6 teaspoons stevia blend	30 ml
or 12 packets of stevia	
1 egg	1
¼ teaspoon nutmeg	1.25 ml
¼ teaspoon ginger	1.25 ml
½ teaspoon cinnamon	2.5 ml
1 cup whipped cream (see index)	235 ml
1 unbaked pie shell (see Index)	1

In a blender, whip cream cheese and pumpkin until smooth. Add heavy cream, stevia, egg, and spices and continue blending until smooth.

Prepare pie shell (see index) as instructed. Pour pumpkin mix into pie shell. Bake at 350 degrees for 35-45 minutes or until center is firm. Remove from oven and cool. Top with whipped cream.

Makes 8 servings

NUTRITIONAL FACTS PER SERVING: 5G CARBOHYDRATE; 275 CALORIES; 27G TOTAL FAT; 4G PROTEIN • FOOD EXCHANGES: ½ LEAN MEAT; ½ VEGETABLE; 5 FAT

13

Frozen Treats

Frozen Treats

Vanilla Ice Cream

1 cup whole milk	235 ml
1 vanilla bean	1
2 eggs	2
¾ teaspoon Stevioside	3.7 ml
or 6 teaspoons stevia blend	30 ml
or 12 packets of stevia	
1 pinch salt	1 pinch
2 cups heavy cream	475 ml
1 teaspoon vanilla extract	5 ml

In a large pot, scald milk with vanilla bean, stirring constantly. In a separate bowl, beat eggs well. While whisking eggs, slowly add one cup of hot milk and mix until well blended. Pour egg mixture into hot milk while whisking milk. Add stevia and stir until dissolved. Remove vanilla bean, slice open lengthwise and remove seeds. Return seeds to milk mixture. Remove from heat and stir in salt, cream and vanilla. Cover and refrigerate. When cool, transfer to ice cream maker and freeze according to manufacturer's instructions.

Yield: six 1-cup servings

NUTRITIONAL FACTS PER SERVING: 4G CARBOHYDRATE; 322 CALORIES; 32G TOTAL FAT; 5G PROTEIN • FOOD EXCHANGES: ½ LEAN MEAT; 6½ FAT

Traditional Gelato "Buon Talenti"

An Italian treat without the guilt.

2 cups whole milk	475 ml
½ teaspoon stevioside	2.5 ml
or 4 teaspoons stevia blend	20 ml
or 8 packets of stevia	
4 large egg yolks	4 large
¾ cup heavy cream	175 ml
½ teaspoon amaretto	2.5 ml

In a saucepan, bring milk and stevia to a light simmer. When stevia is dissolved, place milk in the refrigerator until cool.

In another bowl, beat egg yolks and then in a slow stream, slowly add the hot milk mixture, whisking constantly. Return the mixture back to the saucepan. Heat mixture over low heat. Using a thermometer, stir until it reaches 170 degrees. DO NOT BOIL. Place the saucepan into a bowl of ice water to cool. Stir in cream and amaretto.

Once the custard has cooled, place into an ice-cream maker and freeze according to the manufacturer's instructions. Serve immediately. You can place gelato into freezer when the ice cream maker has completed the cycle but do not let harden for more than 2 hours.

Makes four 1-cup servings

NUTRITIONAL FACTS PER SERVING: 7G CARBOHYDRATE; 290 CALORIES; 26G TOTAL FAT; 8G PROTEIN • FOOD EXCHANGES: ½ LEAN MEAT; 5 FAT

Chocolate Ice Cream

¾ teaspoon stevioside	4 ml
or 6 teaspoons stevia blend	30 ml
or 12 packets of stevia	
5 tablespoons cocoa powder	75 ml
½ teaspoon guar gum (optional)	2.5 ml
⅛ teaspoon salt	½ ml
1 cup milk	235 ml
1 egg, beaten	1
2 cups heavy whipping cream	475 ml
1 teaspoon vanilla extract	5 ml

Combine stevia, cocoa, guar gum, and salt in a saucepan. Gradually stir in milk, and cook over medium heat, stirring constantly, until mixture begins to simmer. Gradually stir 1 cup of the hot mixture into the beaten egg. Stirring constantly, gradually pour egg mixture into remaining hot milk mixture. Continue cooking and stirring over low heat until slightly thickened. Remove from heat and let cool. Add whipping cream and vanilla. Cover and refrigerate. When cold, transfer to ice cream maker and freeze according to manufacturer's instructions.

Makes six 1-cup servings

NUTRITIONAL FACTS PER SERVING: 7G CARBOHYDRATE; 322 CALORIES; 32G TOTAL FAT; 5G PROTEIN • FOOD EXCHANGES: 6½ FAT

VARIATIONS:

Chocolate Chocolate Ice Cream: Prepare Dark Chocolate Candy (see Index) but keep candy melted. When ice cream becomes semihard, stream the chocolate candy into the chocolate ice cream and then finish freezing process. Adds 1½ carbohydrates per serving.

Chocolate Chocolate Mint Ice Cream: Prepare Chocolate Mint recipe (see Index) but keep candy melted. When ice cream becomes semihard, stream the chocolate mint candy into the chocolate ice cream and then finish freezing process. Adds 1½ carbohydrates per serving.

Cappuccino Semifreddo

1½ cups strongly brewed coffee	355 ml
1½ cups whole milk	355 ml
⅜ teaspoon stevioside	1.85 ml
or 3 teaspoons stevia blend	15 ml
or 6 packets of stevia	
2 teaspoons cocoa powder	10 ml
1½ cups heavy cream	355 ml

Cool coffee in an ice/water bath or in refrigerator until very cold. In a blender, blend milk, stevioside and cocoa together. Add coffee and blend well.

Whip cream until soft peaks form. Gently fold in coffee mixture. Place mixture into freezer for about 1 hour. Mixture should start to become firm. Coffee and cream may begin to separate so refold mixture gently to keep emulsified. Allow mixture to freeze for about another hour or until just slightly firm. Serve immediately.

Yields nine ½-cup servings

NUTRITIONAL FACTS PER SERVING: 3G CARBOHYDRATE; 163 CALORIES; 16G TOTAL FAT; 2G PROTEIN • FOOD EXCHANGES: 3 FAT

Jalapeño Ice Cream

A delicious yet spicy treat.

Vanilla Ice Cream (see Index)	
2 teaspoons jalapeño, finely chopped	10 ml
½ cup water	120 ml
⅜ teaspoon stevioside	1.8 ml
or 3 teaspoons stevia blend	15 ml
or 6 packets of stevia	
1 teaspoon lime peel	5 ml
¼ teaspoon guar gum	1.25 ml
2 kiwi fruit, peeled & chopped	2
1 tablespoon lime juice	15 ml
¼ cup raspberries	60 ml

During the preparation of the ice cream, add the chopped jalapeno with the vanilla bean.

In a small saucepan, bring water, stevia, lime peel and guar gum to a boil. Remove from heat and allow to cool and thicken. In a food processor, blend kiwi fruit and lime juice until smooth. Add water mixture. Refrigerate until cold.

In 6 dessert bowls, spoon kiwi sauce into bottom of bowls. Scoop 1 cup of ice cream into each bowl. Garnish with raspberries.

Makes six 1-cup servings

NUTRITIONAL FACTS PER SERVING: 9G CARBOHYDRATE; 342 CALORIES; 32G TOTAL FAT; 5G PROTEIN • FOOD EXCHANGES: ½ LEAN MEAT; ½ FRUIT; 6½ FAT

Avocado Ice Cream

This recipe may sound weird but it is yummy.

4 cups heavy cream	1 liter
1½ teaspoons stevioside	7½ ml
or 12 teaspoons stevia blend	60 ml
or 24 packets of stevia	
1 vanilla bean	1
2 eggs	2
1 egg yolk	1
3 small avocados	3 small
¼ cup limejuice	60 ml

Combine cream, stevia and vanilla bean in a saucepan. Gently bring cream to a boil over medium heat while stirring constantly. Remove from heat. Remove vanilla bean and slice in half lengthwise. Return seeds to saucepan.

In a large bowl, beat eggs until frothy. While beating, slowly add in 1 cup of the hot cream mixture and beat well. Slowly pour egg mixture into saucepan with remaining hot cream. Cook over medium heat and whisk slowly to ensure that mixture does not burn. Do not allow the mixture to boil. Remove from heat cool in refrigerator.

In a food processor, puree peeled, pitted avocados and lime juice. Stir puree into custard mixture. Transfer custard into ice cream maker and follow manufacturer's instructions.

Makes about eight 1-cup servings

NUTRITIONAL FACTS PER SERVING: 7G CARBOHYDRATE; 372 CALORIES; 38G TOTAL FAT; 4G PROTEIN • FOOD EXCHANGES: ½ LEAN MEAT; 6½ FAT

Citrus Ice Cream

2 cups heavy cream	475 ml
1½ teaspoons stevioside	7½ ml
or 12 teaspoons stevia blend	60 ml
or 24 packets of stevia	
⅓ cup lemon juice	80 ml
⅓ cup orange juice	80 ml
1 tablespoon orange peel	15 ml

In a large bowl, combine cream and stevia and stir until dissolved. Add juices and peel. Mix well. Pour mixture into ice cream machine and follow manufacturer's instructions.

Yields six ½-cup servings

NUTRITIONAL FACTS PER SERVING: 5G CARBOHYDRATE; 284 CALORIES; 29G TOTAL FAT; 2G PROTEIN • FOOD EXCHANGES: 6 FAT

Mango (Papaya) Ice Cream

Probably my favorite ice cream

2 mangos, peeled & pitted	2
or 1 large papaya (depending on season)	
1 teaspoon rum extract	5 ml
⅛ teaspoon stevioside	½ ml
or 1 teaspoon stevia blend	5 ml

or 2 packets of stevia
1 cup evaporated milk	240 ml
1 cup heavy cream	240 ml
½ teaspoon guar gum (optional)	2.5 ml

Peel and pit mangos. Puree fruit in a food processor with remaining ingredients. Pour into ice cream maker and follow manufacturer's instructions.

Makes eight ⅔-cup servings

NUTRITIONAL FACTS PER SERVING: 10G CARBOHYDRATE; 168 CALORIES; 13G TOTAL FAT; 3G PROTEIN • FOOD EXCHANGES: ½ FRUIT; 2½ FAT

Peach Gelato

A very refreshing dish.

1 teaspoon stevioside	5 ml
or 8 teaspoons stevia blend	40 ml
or 16 packets of stevia	
½ cup water	120 ml
1½ pounds peaches	680 g
2 tablespoons lemon juice	30 ml
1 egg white, lightly beaten	1
1 teaspoon vanilla	5 ml

In a heavy saucepan, dissolve stevia into water. Cool syrup.

Peel and pit peaches and puree smooth in a food processor. You need only 2 cups of the peach puree. Add the puree to the stevia syrup and stir in lemon juice. Chill peach mixture until very cold. Stir in egg white and vanilla and place mixture into an ice-cream machine. Follow manufacturer's instructions. Serve immediately.

Makes eight ½-cup servings

NUTRITIONAL FACTS PER SERVING: 8G CARBOHYDRATE; 29 CALORIES; TRACE TOTAL FAT; 1G PROTEIN • FOOD EXCHANGES: ½ FRUIT

Lemon Granita

3 large lemons	3 large
1 cup water	235 ml
½ teaspoon agar	2.5 ml
½ teaspoon stevioside	2.5 ml
or 4 teaspoons stevia blend	20 ml
or 8 packets of stevia	

With a vegetable peeler, remove zest in long pieces from lemons. Squeeze ½ cup of juice from lemons and set aside.

In a heavy saucepan, heat water, agar and stevia, stirring until stevia is dissolved. Stir in zest and transfer syrup to a bowl to cool. Chill syrup, covered, until cold. Discard zest and stir in lemon juice.

Pour mixture into ice cream maker and follow manufacturer's instructions. Serve ½ cup in small dessert bowls garnished with a slice of lemon.

Makes 5 servings

NUTRITIONAL FACTS PER SERVING: 4G CARBOHYDRATE; 7 CALORIES; TRACE TOTAL FAT; TRACE PROTEIN • FOOD EXCHANGES: 0 EXCHANGES

Orange Sherbert

A wonderful summer treat that will remind you of your youth.

1 envelope unflavored gelatin	
1¾ teaspoon stevioside	3.7 ml
or 6 teaspoons stevia blend	30 ml
or 12 packets of stevia	
1 cup warm water	235 ml
1½ cup evaporated milk	355 ml
⅓ cup orange juice	80 ml
1½ cup heavy cream	355 ml
2 tablespoons orange zest	30 ml

Dissolve gelatin and stevia into warm water. Stir in remaining ingredients. Cool in refrigerator until cold. Add to ice cream maker and follow manufacturer's instructions.

Makes 6 servings

NUTRITIONAL FACTS PER SERVING: 9G CARBOHYDRATE; 284 CALORIES; 25G TOTAL FAT; 6G PROTEIN • FOOD EXCHANGES: 5 FAT

Apple Cinnamon Ice Cream

A truly decadent dessert

¼ apple, diced	¼
2 tablespoons butter	30 ml
2 teaspoons cinnamon	10 ml
5 egg yolks	5
3 teaspoons vanilla	15 ml
¼ cup water	60 ml
½ teaspoon stevioside	2.5 ml
or 4 teaspoons stevia blend	20 ml
or 8 packets of stevia	
2 cups heavy cream	475 ml

Saute apple with cinnamon in butter until apple is soft. Set aside and allow to cool. In a mixer, blend egg yolks, vanilla, water and stevia until well mixed. Add heavy cream and beat until fluffy. Add apple mixture and mix well. Transfer to ice cream maker and follow manufacturer's instructions.

Makes 6 servings

NUTRITIONAL FACTS PER SERVING: 5G CARBOHYDRATE; 369 CALORIES; 37G TOTAL FAT; 4G PROTEIN • FOOD EXCHANGES: 7½ FAT

Frozen Lime Pie

Filling:

½ cup milk	120 ml
1 teaspoon stevioside	5 ml
or 8 teaspoons stevia blend	40 ml
or 16 packets of stevia	
2 teaspoons lime peel	10 ml
¼ cup lime juice	60 ml
8 ounces cream cheese	225 g
1 baked crust (see Index)	1

Topping:

1 cup heavy cream	235 ml
⅛ teaspoon stevioside	½ ml
or ½ teaspoon stevia blend	2.5 ml
or 1 packet of stevia	
1 teaspoon vanilla extract	5 ml

In a food processor, blend milk, stevia, lime peel and juice. Gradually add cream cheese. Blend until smooth. Pour into crust. Freeze pie overnight.

Whip heavy cream with ⅛ teaspoon stevioside and vanilla extract until firm peaks form. Garnish pie with whipped cream.

Makes 6 slices

NUTRITIONAL FACTS PER SERVING: 4G CARBOHYDRATE; 246 CALORIES; 24G TOTAL FAT; 4G PROTEIN • FOOD EXCHANGES: ½ LEAN MEAT; 7 FAT

⑭

Sweet Extras

Candies, Dessert Sauces and Tempting Toppings

Sweet Extras

Candies, Dessert Sauces and Tempting Toppings

BERRY PEANUT BUTTER CREAM – 195

CHOCOLATE CREAM CHEESE FROSTING – 203

CHOCOLATE CREAM CHEESE FUDGE – 196

CHOCOLATE MINTS – 199

CHOCOLATE PEANUT BUTTER CREAM – 195

CHOCOLATE WHIPPED CREAM – 203

COCONUT MACAROONS – 200

DARK CHOCOLATE CANDIES – 196

DIPPING CHOCOLATE – 197

FLAVORED WHIPPED CREAM – 203

KAHLÚA FUDGE SAUCE – 201

MAPLE CINNAMON PEANUT BUTTER CREAM – 195

PEANUT BUTTER BALLS – 198

RUM SAUCE – 201

TRUFFLE FUDGE BALLS – 198

VANILLA CREAM CHEESE FROSTING – 202

VANILLA CREAM SAUCE – 202

WHIPPED CREAM – 203

Chocolate Peanut Butter Cream

¾ cup natural Peanut Butter	175 ml
¼ cup vegetable shortening	60 ml
½ ounce unsweetened baking chocolate	15 g
¾ teaspoon stevioside	3.7 ml
or 6 teaspoons stevia blend	30 ml
or 12 packets of stevia	

Pour off excess oil from peanut butter. In a heavy saucepan over low heat, combine peanut butter and vegetable shortening to liquefy. Remove from heat. Add baking chocolate and stevioside. Stir until blended. Transfer to food processor and process on high speed for 3 minutes. Transfer to airtight container and allow to cool to room temperature. Serve as a dip for celery sticks or as a topping for cakes or protein bars.

Makes eight 2-tablespoons servings

NUTRITIONAL FACTS PER SERVING: 5G CARBOHYDRATE; 206 CALORIES; 18G TOTAL FAT; 5G PROTEIN • FOOD EXCHANGES: 1½ FAT

VARIATIONS:

Berry Peanut Butter Cream: omit chocolate and decrease stevioside to ½ teaspoon. Add ¾ teaspoon of strawberry extract and ¾ teaspoon raspberry extract.

Maple Cinnamon Peanut Butter Cream: omit chocolate and decrease stevioside to ½ teaspoon. Add ½ teaspoon maple flavoring and ½ teaspoon of cinnamon. Excellent on waffles and pancakes.

Dark Chocolate Candies

1 ounce parafin wax	28 g
4 ounces unsweetened baking chocolate square	115 g
8 tablespoons butter	120 ml
4 tablespoons heavy cream	60 ml
⅝ teaspoon stevioside	4 ml
or 5 teaspoons stevia blend	25 ml
or 10 packets of stevia	
1¼ teaspoon vanilla extract	6.25 ml
crushed nuts (optional)	

In top of a double boiler, melt chocolate and butter together and gently stir. Heat cream in a saucepan or microwave until it is warm, not hot or cold. Dissolve stevia into the cream. Stir cream and vanilla into the chocolate mix. Pour mixture over wax paper and allow to cool. For variety, add crushed nuts after you add cream and vanilla.

Note on melting chocolate: When using a double boiler, bring the water in the bottom pot to a boil first. Then remove the pot from the heat and place the upper pot over it. Put chocolate and butter in upper pot and stir gently with a wooden or plastic spoon to keep the chocolate shiny. If double boiler remains over heat, the chocolate will cook instead of just melt, which will bring unwanted results.

Makes 4 servings

NUTRITIONAL FACTS PER SERVING: 9G CARBOHYDRATE; 406 CALORIES; 44G TOTAL FAT; 3G PROTEIN • FOOD EXCHANGES: ½ STARCH; 9 FAT

Chocolate Cream Cheese Fudge

16 ounces cream cheese	455 g
2 ounces unsweetened baking chocolate squares	60 g
1 teaspoons stevioside	5 ml
or 8 teaspoons stevia blend	40 ml
or 16 packets of stevia	
½ cup chopped pecans	120 ml
1 teaspoon vanilla extract	5 ml

Cream cheese should be softened to room temperature. In top of double boiler, melt chocolate. Place cream cheese into a mixer and beat until light and fluffy. Add stevia, chopped pecans and vanilla and continue to beat well. Pour in melted chocolate and beat for about 3-5 minutes more. Pour into an 8-inch baking pan that has been lightly greased with butter. Cover and refrigerate overnight. Cut into squares and serve chilled.

Makes 16 servings

NUTRITIONAL FACTS PER SERVING: 3G CARBOHYDRATE; 143 CALORIES; 14G TOTAL FAT; 3G PROTEIN • FOOD EXCHANGES: ½ LEAN MEAT; 2½ FAT

VARIATION

Roll fudge into balls and dip in Dipping Chocolate.

Dipping Chocolate

For making candies or to dip fruit.

1 cup powdered milk	235 ml
⅓ cup cocoa powder	80 ml
2 tablespoons paraffin wax	30 ml
½ teaspoon stevioside	2.5 ml
or 4 teaspoons stevia blend	20 ml
or 8 packets of stevia	
½ cup water	120 ml
1 tablespoon oil	15 ml

Combine powdered milk, cocoa, stevia and wax in a food processor and blend until a soft powder. Pour into the top of a double boiler and add water, stirring to blend. Stir in oil. Place over bottom of double boiler with hot (not boiling) water and stir until all ingredients have dissolved and texture is smooth.

Makes 2 cups of dipping chocolate. Carbohydrate count will vary depending on how this recipe is used.

NUTRITIONAL FACTS PER SERVING: 65G CARBOHYDRATE; 821 CALORIES; 52G TOTAL FAT; 39G PROTEIN • FOOD EXCHANGES: 1 STARCH; ½ LEAN MEAT; 10½ FAT

Peanut Butter Balls

¾ cup chunky peanut butter	175 ml
¼ cup soy flour	60 ml
¼ teaspoon stevioside	1.25 ml
or 2 teaspoons stevia blend	10 ml
or 4 packets of stevia	
½ cup peanuts, dry-roasted, finely chopped	120 ml

In a mixing bowl, blend peanut butter, soy flour and stevia together until well mixed and fluffy. Roll mixture into 24 balls and refrigerate for about 1 hour to harden. Place peanuts into a food processor and pulse-process until nuts are coarsely ground. Roll peanut butter balls in peanuts.

Makes 24 balls

NUTRITIONAL FACTS PER SERVING: 3G CARBOHYDRATE; 69 CALORIES; 6G TOTAL FAT; 3G PROTEIN • FOOD EXCHANGES: ½ LEAN MEAT; 1 FAT

VARIATION:

Dip the peanut butter balls in the dipping chocolate instead of rolling them in the chopped peanuts. Adds about 1 carbohydrate per ball.

Truffle Fudge Balls

⅓ cup butter	80 ml
3 tablespoons evaporated milk	45 ml
1 dash salt	1 dash
½ teaspoon stevioside	2.5 ml
or 4 teaspoons stevia blend	20 ml
or 8 packets of stevia	
1 teaspoon vanilla	5 ml
¼ cup cocoa powder	60 ml
Dipping Chocolate (see Index)	

Cream butter, milk, salt, stevia and vanilla until fluffy. Stir in cocoa. Knead dough until smooth. Form into small balls. Dip each ball into dipping chocolate and then allow to cool. Repeat procedure one more time.

Makes 60 balls

NUTRITIONAL FACTS PER SERVING: 1G CARBOHYDRATE; 25 CALORIES; 2G TOTAL FAT; 1G PROTEIN • FOOD EXCHANGES: ½ FAT

Chocolate Mints

1 ounce parafin wax	28 g
1½ ounces unsweetened baking chocolate	45 g
2 tablespoons butter	30 ml
1 tablespoon heavy cream	15 ml
⅝ teaspoon stevioside	4 ml
or 5 teaspoons stevia blend	25 ml
or 10 packets of stevia	
½ teaspoon vanilla	2.5 ml
½ teaspoon peppermint extract	2.5 ml

In top of double boiler, melt chocolate, wax, and butter. In a bowl, mix heavy cream, stevia, vanilla, and peppermint extract. While whisking the chocolate constantly, add heavy cream mixture in a steady stream. Continue stirring until mixture is smooth. Pour into a waxed paper-lined dish or into candy molds. Chill until chocolate sets.

Makes 8 mints.

NUTRITIONAL FACTS PER SERVING: 2G CARBOHYDRATE; 61 CALORIES; 6G TOTAL FAT; 1G PROTEIN • FOOD EXCHANGES: 1½ FAT

Coconut Macaroons

1⅓ cups unsweetened coconut meat, shredded	315 ml
¼ teaspoon stevioside	1 ml
or 2 teaspoons stevia blend	10 ml
or 4 packets of stevia	
1 tablespoon soy flour	15 ml
⅛ teaspoon salt	½ ml
2 egg whites	2
¾ teaspoon almond extract	3.7 ml

In a large bowl, combine coconut, stevia, flour and salt. Stir in egg whites and almond extract. Using a large spoon, drop heaping spoonfuls onto a greased cookie sheet to make 12 cookies. Bake at 325 degrees for 20 to 25 minutes, when edge of cookies turn golden brown. Remove from cookie sheet and allow to cool.

Makes 12 macaroons

NUTRITIONAL FACTS PER SERVING: 2G CARBOHYDRATE; 64 CALORIES; 6G TOTAL FAT; 1G PROTEIN • FOOD EXCHANGES: 1 FAT

Kahlúa Fudge Sauce

6 ounces unsweetened baking chocolate squares	170 g
½ teaspoon stevioside	2 ½ ml
or 4 teaspoons stevia blend	20 ml
or 8 packets of stevia	
¼ cup Kahlua (see Index)	60 ml
6 tablespoons heavy cream	90 ml

In top of double boiler, gently melt chocolate. In another saucepan, dissolve stevia into kahlua and cream. In a slow steady stream, stir in melted chocolate and stir until smooth. Serve warm over ice cream, cake, etc.

Makes six 2-tablespoon servings

NUTRITIONAL FACTS PER SERVING: 14G CARBOHYDRATE; 238 CALORIES; 21G TOTAL FAT; 3G PROTEIN • FOOD EXCHANGES: ½ STARCH; 4 FAT

Rum Sauce

3 cups heavy cream	710 ml
1 teaspoons stevioside	5 ml
or 8 teaspoons stevia blend	40 ml
or 16 packets of stevia	
1½ cups rum	355 ml
or 2 tablespoons rum extract	30 ml

In a saucepan, gently heat cream with stevia. While stirring, bring to a boil and then immediately remove from heat. Stir in rum or extract and serve over ice cream, angel food cake or fresh fruit.

Makes 8 servings

NUTRITIONAL FACTS PER SERVING: 2G CARBOHYDRATE; 408 CALORIES; 33G TOTAL FAT; 2G PROTEIN • FOOD EXCHANGES: 6½ FAT

Vanilla Creme Sauce

3 each eggs, beaten	3 each
2 cups heavy cream	475 ml
⅜ teaspoon stevioside	1.8 ml
or 3 teaspoons stevia blend	15 ml
or 6 packets of stevia	
1 teaspoon vanilla	5 ml

In a medium saucepan, combine all ingredients and cook over low heat. Stir constantly until sauce thickens (sauce should thickly coat a spoon). Remove from heat and pour over pancakes, crepes, fruit, etc. Or store in refrigerator in an airtight container until needed.

Makes 6 servings

NUTRITIONAL FACTS PER SERVING: 3G CARBOHYDRATE; 308 CALORIES; 32G TOTAL FAT; 4G PROTEIN • FOOD EXCHANGES: ½ LEAN MEAT; 6 FAT

Variations:

It is very easy to flavor this sauce by simply adding one teaspoon of your favorite flavored extract to this sauce when you are cooking it.

Vanilla Cream Cheese Frosting

16 ounces cream cheese at room temperature	455 g
¾ teaspoon stevioside	3.7 ml
or 6 teaspoons stevia blend	30 ml
or 12 packets of stevia	
3 tablespoon heavy cream	45 ml
1 teaspoon vanilla extract	5 ml

In a medium mixing bowl, beat cream cheese, stevia, heavy cream and vanilla until light and fluffy.

Makes about 2 cups

NUTRITIONAL FACTS PER ENTIRE RECIPE: 15G CARBOHYDRATE; 1750 CALORIES; 175G TOTAL FAT; 35G PROTEIN • FOOD EXCHANGES: 5 LEAN MEAT; 32½ FAT

VARIATION:

Chocolate Cream Cheese Icing: Add ⅓ cup Dutch Process Cocoa and whip mixture until light and fluffy. Adds a total of 12 carbohydrates for the entire recipe.

Whipped Cream

1 cup heavy cream	235 ml
⅛ teaspoon stevioside	½ ml
or 1 teaspoon stevia blend	5 ml
or 2 packets of stevia	
1 teaspoon vanilla	5 ml

In a bowl, combine whipping cream, stevia blend, and vanilla. Beat on medium speed until soft peaks form.

Yield: eight ¼-cup servings

NUTRITIONAL FACTS PER SERVING: TRACE CARBOHYDRATE; 4 CALORIES; TRACE TOTAL FAT; TRACE PROTEIN • FOOD EXCHANGES: 0 EXCHANGES

VARIATIONS:

Chocolate Whipped Cream: Add 2 tablespoons of cocoa powder prior to whipping up the heavy cream.

Flavored Whipped Cream: Add 1 teaspoon of your favorite extract during the whipping process.

15

Flavor Enhancers

Spice Blends, Condiments, Sauces, and Relishes

Flavor Enhancers

Spice Blends, Condiments, Sauces, and Relishes

One of the most frequent complaints about the low-carb lifestyle is the lack of variety in the diet. This chapter may be the single most important chapter because it offers the quickest, easiest and most delicious ways to add variety to one's diet. A simple chicken breast becomes exotic when grilled after being rubbed with the Moroccan Spice blend. An omelet becomes a bit southwestern when covered with cheese and Picante sauce. You can even mix a little Sweet & Spicy Texas rub in with your shredded cheese then fry it up for an added "Texas Kick." Let your culinary imagination go wild.

Always keep a bottle of sugar-free catsup, BBQ sauce and Picante Sauce in the refrigerator and you will avoid the temptation to use sugar filled commercial versions. An added bonus is that stevia is a flavor enhancer giving all of your condiments, sauces, relishes and spice blends a stronger, fuller flavor.

Chinese Five-Spice Blend

4 tablespoons fennel seeds	60 ml
12 whole star anise	12 whole
4 tablespoons cinnamon stick, crushed	60 ml
4 tablespoons cloves	60 ml
4 tablespoons black peppercorns	60 ml
1 teaspoon green stevia powder	5 ml

In a mortar, grind each spice (separately). Then, add all of the crushed spices back to the mortar and grind until the mixture is well mixed. Add stevia and store in an airtight container. For extra flavor, prior to grinding the spices, gently heat the seeds and peppercorns over low heat in a clean, dry skillet.

NUTRITIONAL FACTS FOR ENTIRE RECIPE: 162G CARBOHYDRATE; 772 CALORIES: 26G TOTAL FAT; 29G PROTEIN • FOOD EXCHANGES: 10½ STARCH; 1 LEAN MEAT; 4½ FAT

Chocolate Chili Powder

A wonderful alternative to plain chili powder.

½ cup pumpkin seeds, roasted	120 ml
3 each red chiles	3
1 tablespoon cocoa powder	15 ml
1 chipotle pepper, toasted	1
1 tablespoon cumin seed	15 ml
1 tablespoon coriander	15 ml
1 tablespoon oregano	15 ml
1 teaspoon cinnamon	5 ml
1 teaspoon allspice	5 ml
1 teaspoon green stevia powder	5 ml

In a mortar, grind each spice (separately). Then add all of the crushed spices back to the mortar and grind until the mixture is well mixed. Add stevia and store in an airtight container. For extra flavor, prior to grinding the spices, gently heat the seeds and peppercorns over low heat in a clean skillet.

NUTRITIONAL FACTS FOR ENTIRE RECIPE: 50G CARBOHYDRATE; 293 CALORIES; 9G TOTAL FAT; 13G PROTEIN • FOOD EXCHANGES: 2 STARCH; ½ LEAN MEAT; 4 VEGETABLE; 1½ FAT

Curry Powder

You'll never buy curry powder again after you have made your own.

1 tablespoon black peppercorns	15 ml
2 teaspoons turmeric	10 ml
1 tablespoon ginger, dried	15 ml
1 tablespoon coriander	15 ml
1 tablespoon cumin seed	15 ml
1 teaspoon celery seed	5 ml
1 teaspoon green stevia powder	5 ml

In a mortar, grind all ingredients together. Store in an airtight container. For better flavor, gently heat seeds and peppercorns prior to grinding.

NUTRITIONAL FACTS PER ENTIRE RECIPE: 22G CARBOHYDRATE; 111 CALORIES; 3G TOTAL FAT; 4G PROTEIN • FOOD EXCHANGES: 1½ STARCH; ½ FAT

Masala Spice Blend

⅓ whole nutmeg	⅓ whole
½ teaspoon fennel seed	2.5 ml
1 teaspoon black peppercorns	5 ml
1 teaspoon cumin seed	5 ml
1 teaspoon cinnamon	5 ml
1 tablespoon cardamom	15 ml
1 teaspoon whole cloves	5 ml
1 teaspoon green stevia powder	5 ml

In a mortar, grind all ingredients together. Store in an airtight container. For better flavor, gently heat seeds and peppercorns prior to grinding.

NUTRITIONAL FACTS PER ENTIRE RECIPE: 13G CARBOHYDRATE; 69 CALORIES; 3G TOTAL FAT; 2G PROTEIN • FOOD EXCHANGES: 1 STARCH; ½ FAT

Moroccan Spice Blend

4 teaspoons peppercorns	20 ml
1 teaspoon cumin	5 ml
6 whole cloves	6 whole
1 teaspoon turmeric	5 ml
1 teaspoon cinnamon	5 ml
2 rose buds, dried	2
½ teaspoon cardamom	2.5 ml
1 teaspoon ginger	5 ml
1 tablespoon coriander seed	15 ml
1 teaspoon mace	5 ml
1 teaspoon green stevia powder	5 ml

In a mortar, grind each spice (separately). Then, add all of the crushed spices back to the mortar and grind until the mixture is well mixed. Add stevia and store in an airtight container. For extra flavor, prior to grinding the spices, gently heat the seeds and peppercorns over low heat in a clean skillet.

NUTRITIONAL FACTS PER ENTIRE RECIPE: 49G CARBOHYDRATE; 242 CALORIES; 11G TOTAL FAT; 7G PROTEIN • FOOD EXCHANGES: 3 STARCH; 2 FAT

Sweet & Spicy Texas Rub

A special treat for anyone who loves Texas ribs.

⅛ teaspoon stevioside	½ ml
1 teaspoon stevia blend	5 ml
or 2 packets of stevia	
6 tablespoons paprika	90 ml
1½ teaspoons cayenne	7.5 ml
1 tablespoon onion powder	15 ml
2 tablespoons black pepper	30 ml
2 tablespoons chili powder	30 ml
2 tablespoons garlic powder	30 ml
2 tablespoons salt	30 ml

Combine all ingredients and store in an airtight container. Use as a rub for grilled meats. If you like it hot, double the cayenne, but beware, it does get hot.

NUTRITIONAL FACTS PER ENTIRE RECIPE: 10G CARBOHYDRATE; 48 CALORIES; 1G TOTAL FAT; 2G PROTEIN • FOOD EXCHANGES: ½ STARCH; ½ FAT

Sweet Spice Blend

2 teaspoons mace	10 ml
2 tablespoons coriander seed	30 ml
2 tablespoons orange zest, dried	30 ml
12 whole cloves	12 whole
2 tablespoons cinnamon sticks, lightly crushed	30 ml
24 allspice berries	24
1 teaspoon cardamom	5 ml
2 slices ginger, dried	2 slices
⅛ teaspoon stevioside	½ ml
or 1 teaspoon stevia blend	5 ml
or 2 packets of stevia	

In a mortar, grind each spice (separately). Then, add all of the crushed spices back to the mortar and grind until the mixture is well mixed. Store in an airtight container.

For extra flavor, prior to grinding the spices, gently heat the seeds and peppercorns over low heat in a clean skillet.

NUTRITIONAL FACTS PER ENTIRE RECIPE: 195G CARBOHYDRATE; 812 CALORIES; 33G TOTAL FAT; 17G PROTEIN • FOOD EXCHANGES: 12½ STARCH; 6½ FAT

Tangy Catsup

A spicy version of your everyday catsup.

1 cup apple cider vinegar	240 ml
1 teaspoon ground cinnamon	5 ml
1 teaspoon celery seed	5 ml
48 ounces canned tomatoes, diced	1,360 g
½ cup onions, minced	120 ml
½ teaspoon red pepper	2.5 ml
⅜ teaspoon stevioside	1.85 ml
or 3 teaspoons stevia blend	15 ml
or 6 packets of stevia	
2 tablespoons tomato paste	30 ml

In a small saucepan, stir together vinegar, cinnamon, and celery seed; bring to a boil. Set aside. In a heavy stockpot or large saucepan, mix together remaining ingredients; bring to a boil, stirring occasionally. Reduce heat. Add vinegar mix. Simmer for 30 minutes, stirring occasionally. In small batches, puree in blender or food processor. Return to pot; simmer, stirring occasionally, until thick.

Spicy Catsup: Add 3 tablespoons of hot sauce during the simmering stage.

Makes 64 servings

NUTRITIONAL FACTS PER SERVING: 1G CARBOHYDRATE; 6 CALORIES; TRACE TOTAL FAT; TRACE PROTEIN • FOOD EXCHANGES: 0 EXCHANGES

Traditional Catsup

1 tablespoon arrowroot	15 ml
1 teaspoon water	5 ml
2 cups tomato sauce	475 ml
¼ cup apple cider vinegar	60 ml
⅛ teaspoon stevioside	½ ml
or 1 teaspoon stevia blend	5 ml
or 2 packets of stevia	
¼ teaspoon onion powder	1.25 ml

In a small cup, mix arrowroot and water. Stir until dissolved. In a large saucepan, combine all ingredients; mix well. Stirring constantly, bring to a gentle boil. Still stirring constantly, reduce heat and simmer to desired thickness. Refrigerate until needed.

Makes about 1½ cups (24 servings)

NUTRITIONAL FACTS PER SERVING: 2G CARBOHYDRATE; 8 CALORIES; TRACE TOTAL FAT; TRACE PROTEIN • FOOD EXCHANGES: 0 EXCHANGES

Cocktail Sauce

1 cup Traditional Catsup (see Index)	235 ml
3 tablespoons onion, grated	45 ml
3 tablespoons prepared horseradish	45 ml
2 tablespoons lemon juice	30 ml
2 tablespoons tarragon, minced	30 ml
1 dash Tabasco sauce, to taste	1 dash

Whisk all ingredients in a medium bowl to blend. Cover and refrigerate at least 1 hour. For a bit more spice try substituting the traditional catsup with the Tangy Catsup (see Index).

Makes 1½ cups (about 6 servings).

NUTRITIONAL FACTS PER SERVING: 10G CARBOHYDRATE; 42 CALORIES; TRACE TOTAL FAT; 2G PROTEIN • FOOD EXCHANGES: 1 VEGETABLE

Picante Sauce

24 ounces canned tomatoes, finely diced	680 g
6 ounces tomato juice, reserved from can	170 g
1 small onion, chopped	1 small
4 ounces green chili peppers, finely chopped	115 g
2 tablespoons cilantro, minced	30 ml
1 tablespoon lime juice	15 ml
¼ teaspoon stevioside	1.25 ml
or 2 teaspoons stevia blend	10 ml
or 4 packets of stevia	
1 teaspoon salt	5 ml
1 teaspoon pepper	5 ml
1 jalapeño, finely chopped	1

In a bowl, combine all ingredients; mix well. Refrigerate at least 2 hours to blend flavors.

Makes about 4 cups (16 servings)

Note: If you like it HOT, add an extra jalapeño or two; or, for the really brave (or insane), add a finely chopped Habañero pepper.

NUTRITIONAL FACTS PER SERVING: 4G CARBOHYDRATE; 16 CALORIES; TRACE TOTAL FAT; 1G PROTEIN • FOOD EXCHANGES: ½ VEGETABLE

Mexicali Sauce

¼ teaspoon stevioside	1.25 ml
or 2 teaspoons stevia blend	10 ml
or 4 packets of stevia	
½ cup Picante Sauce (see Index)	120 ml
1 tablespoon tomato paste	15 ml
1 tablespoon Dijon mustard	15 ml

In a bowl, dissolve stevia into picante sauce. Mix remaining ingredients into picante sauce. Stir until well mixed. Keep refrigerated until needed. Use as a baste or sauce.

Makes about ½ cup

NUTRITIONAL FACTS PER SERVING: 6G CARBOHYDRATE; 32 CALORIES; 1G TOTAL FAT; 1G PROTEIN • FOOD EXCHANGES: 1 VEGETABLE

Cilantro Sauce

One of my personal favorites over grilled chicken.

½ cup butter, melted	120 ml
8 ounces chilies	230 g
1 cup cilantro	235 ml
2 tablespoons lime juice	30 ml
⅛ teaspoon stevioside	½ ml
or 1 teaspoon stevia blend	5 ml
or 2 packets of stevia	
⅓ cup dry white wine	80 ml

Puree all ingredients together in a food processor. Pour mixture into a saucepan and bring to a boil until mixture is reduced by half. Stir continuously. Serve over grilled or roasted chicken.

NUTRITIONAL FACTS PER SERVING: 5G CARBOHYDRATE; 239 CALORIES; 23G TOTAL FAT; 2G PROTEIN • FOOD EXCHANGES: 4½ FAT

Black Bean Salsa

⅛ teaspoon stevioside	½ ml
or 1 teaspoon stevia blend	5 ml
or 2 packets of stevia	
3 tablespoons lime juice	45 ml
3 tomatoes, finely diced	3 medium
4 ounces black beans, canned, drained	115 g
4 ounces green chilies, chopped	115 g
3 tablespoons cilantro, finely chopped	45 ml
1 small onion, finely chopped	1 small
1 clove garlic, minced	1 clove
1 medium jalapeño, finely chopped	1 medium
¼ teaspoon cinnamon	1.25 ml
to taste salt and pepper	to taste

In a small bowl, dissolve stevia into the lime juice. Set aside. In another bowl, combine all of the other ingredients. Add lime mixture; mix well. Refrigerate at least 2 hours before serving.

Makes about 4½ cups (18 servings)

Note: If you like it hot, add an extra jalapeno or two.

NUTRITIONAL FACTS PER SERVING: 6G CARBOHYDRATE; 32 CALORIES; TRACE TOTAL FAT; 2G PROTEIN • FOOD EXCHANGES: ½ STARCH; ½ VEGETABLE

Traditional Barbecue Sauce

½ small onion, minced	½ small
1 clove garlic, minced	1 clove
2 tablespoons butter	30 ml
1 cup Traditional Catsup (see Index)	235 ml
¼ cup bourbon (optional)	60 ml
⅛ teaspoon stevioside	½ ml
or 1 teaspoon stevia blend	5 ml
or 2 packets of stevia	
2 tablespoons Worcestershire sauce	30 ml
1 teaspoon mustard powder	5 ml
1 teaspoon salt	5 ml
1 teaspoon chili powder	5 ml
1 teaspoon Tabasco sauce	5 ml

In a heavy saucepan, sauté onion and garlic in butter until onion is clear. Add remaining ingredients. Bring to a boil and simmer 10 minutes. Use as a baste on meats for grilling. Simmer 10-15 minutes longer to reduce to a thicker sauce for serving with cooked meat.

Makes 2 cups (twenty-eight 1-tablespoon servings).

NUTRITIONAL FACTS PER SERVING: 3G CARBOHYDRATE; 23 CALORIES; 1G TOTAL FAT; TRACE PROTEIN • FOOD EXCHANGES: 0 EXCHANGES

Mayo-BBQ Sauce

½ cup Barbecue Sauce (see Index)   120 ml
1 cup mayonnaise   235 ml

Combine ingredients and use as a glaze over grilled meat.

Makes ten 2½-tablespoon servings

NUTRITIONAL FACTS PER SERVING: 2G CARBOHYDRATE; 167 CALORIES; 19G TOTAL
FAT; TRACE PROTEIN • FOOD EXCHANGES: 1½ FAT

Mustard Barbecue Sauce

*If you have ever had Carolina BBQ, then you know how wonderful this
sauce is!*

1 cup yellow mustard   235 ml
⅔ cup apple cider vinegar   160 ml
1 tablespoon worcestershire sauce   15 ml
1½ cups Traditional Catsup (see Index)   355 ml
½ teaspoon maple flavoring   2.5 ml
2 tablespoons olive oil   30 ml
½ teaspoon black pepper   2.5 ml
1 teaspoon stevioside   5 ml
   or 8 teaspoons stevia blend   40 ml
   or 16 packets of stevia

Combine all ingredients in a medium sauce pan. Simmer over medium
heat, stirring occasionally, until sauce is well blended and hot. Remove
from heat; allow to cool. Keep refrigerated until needed. Use as a baste or
sauce.

Makes about 2 cups. (4 servings)

NUTRITIONAL FACTS PER SERVING: 7G CARBOHYDRATE; 114 CALORIES; 9G TOTAL FAT;
3G PROTEIN • FOOD EXCHANGES: ½ LEAN MEAT; 1½ FAT; ½ OTHER CARBOHYDRATES

Brown Aspic Sauce

2 tablespoons butter	30 ml
1 envelope gelatin	1 envelope
1 cup beef stock	235 ml
⅛ teaspoon stevioside	.5 ml
or 1 teaspoons stevia blend	5 ml
or 2 packets of stevia	
3 tablespoons soy sauce	45 ml

In saucepan melt butter, stir in gelatin dissolved in beef stock, stevia and soy sauce. Cook and stir until thickened and translucent.

Note: This sauce is very versatile. Use as a glaze over ham as a honey replacement. Add sliced mushrooms and serve over cube steak or hamburgers. Serve chilled as a jelly glaze.

Yield: twelve 1-cup servings.

NUTRITIONAL FACTS PER SERVING: TRACE CARBOHYDRATE; 21 CALORIES; 2G TOTAL FAT; TRACE PROTEIN • FOOD EXCHANGES: ½ FAT

Sweet Stevia Pesto

6 ounces Parmesan cheese	180 g
2 cloves garlic	2 cloves
½ cup olive oil	120 ml
2 cups fresh basil leaves, packed	480 ml
½ cup cilantro leaves, whole	120 ml
½ cup fresh parsley	120 ml
1 teaspoon stevioside	5 ml
or 7 teaspoons stevia blend	35 ml
or 14 packets of stevia	

Grate Parmesan cheese in food processor or blender and set aside. With chopping blade in place, puree garlic cloves in olive oil and allow to stand for 15 minutes. Meanwhile, wash and thoroughly dry basil, cilantro and parsley. Add herbs and stevia to olive oil mixture in food processor/blender and puree. Add grated cheese and additional olive oil, if needed.

Traditionally, pesto is served with pasta, but there are many options, such as over sliced, grilled chicken.

Makes 6 servings

NUTRITIONAL FACTS PER SERVING: 2G CARBOHYDRATE; 293 CALORIES; 27G TOTAL FAT; 12G PROTEIN • FOOD EXCHANGES: 1½ LEAN MEAT; 4 FAT

Stevia Dolce Sauce

5 cloves garlic, unpeeled	5 cloves
1 onion, chopped	1
3 tablespoons olive oil	45 ml
4 tablespoons Chocolate Chili Powder (see Index)	60 ml
⅛ teaspoon stevioside	½ ml
or 1 teaspoon stevia blend	5 ml
or 2 packets of stevia	
16 ounces tomatoes, chopped	455 g
1 cup chicken stock	235 ml
1 cup orange juice	235 ml

In an ungreased skillet, toast garlic over medium heat. Stir often. Remove from skillet, peel and chop. In the skillet, sauté onion and garlic in oil until tender and onions are clear. Add chili powder, stevia, tomatoes, chicken stock and juice. Simmer for about 20-30 minutes or until sauce has reduced by ⅓ and thickened. Salt and pepper to taste.

Serve sauce with sliced grilled chicken, beef or pork.

Makes 6 servings

NUTRITIONAL FACTS PER SERVING: 10G CARBOHYDRATE; 107 CALORIES; 7G TOTAL FAT; 1G PROTEIN • FOOD EXCHANGES: 1 VEGETABLE; ½ FRUIT; 1½ FAT

Red Pepper Sauce

Wonderful on omelets.

1 onion, chopped	1
2 red pepper, chopped	2
2 tablespoons olive oil	30 ml
⅛ teaspoon stevioside	½ ml
or 1 teaspoon stevia blend	5 ml
or 2 packets of stevia	
16 ounces canned tomatoes	455 g
½ teaspoon paprika	2.5 ml
¼ teaspoon chili powder	1.25 ml
to taste salt and pepper	to taste

Sauté onion and pepper in oil until soft. Add all remaining ingredients and simmer covered for 30 minutes. Allow to cool and then puree in a food processor.

Serve over protein pasta or sliced chicken breasts.

Makes 4 servings

NUTRITIONAL FACTS PER SERVING: 11G CARBOHYDRATE; 109 CALORIES; 7G TOTAL FAT; 2G PROTEIN • FOOD EXCHANGES: 2 VEGETABLE; 1½ FAT

Sweet & Sour Sauce

¾ cup water	175 ml
⅓ cup apple cider vinegar	80 ml
⅓ cup Traditional Catsup (see index)	80ml
⅝ teaspoon stevioside	3 ml
or 5 teaspoons stevia blend	25 ml
or 10 packets of stevia	
1 tablespoon soy sauce	15 ml
2 tablespoons arrowroot	30 ml

In a heavy saucepan, combine water, vinegar, catsup, stevia and soy sauce. Dissolve arrowroot in 1 tablespoon of water. Stir in cornstarch. Over medium heat, cook, stirring constantly, until thick and bubbly, then continue cooking and stirring for 1 minute more. Remove from heat. Serve hot.

Makes about 1 cup (4 servings)

NUTRITIONAL FACTS PER SERVING: 13G CARBOHYDRATE; 52 CALORIES; TRACE TOTAL FAT; 2G PROTEIN • FOOD EXCHANGES: 1½ VEGETABLE

Hoisin Sauce

Hoisin sauce is a traditional Chinese sauce made from peanuts. Delicious with a lot of flavor.

⅛ teaspoon white pepper	½ ml
4 tablespoons soy sauce	60 ml
2 tablespoons peanut butter	30 ml
⅛ teaspoon stevioside	½ ml
or 1 teaspoon stevia blend	5 ml
or 2 packets of stevia	
2 teaspoons vinegar	10 ml
1 clove garlic, minced	1 clove
2 teaspoons sesame seed oil	10 ml
½ teaspoon hot sauce	2.5 ml

In a bowl, mix all ingredients together until well incorporated. Refrigerate for up to 2 weeks.

Makes 4 servings

NUTRITIONAL FACTS PER SERVING: **4G CARBOHYDRATE;** 59 CALORIES; 4G TOTAL FAT; 3G PROTEIN • FOOD EXCHANGES: ½ VEGETABLE; ½ FAT

Hoisin BBQ Sauce

1 cup Hoisin Sauce (see Index)	235 ml
2 tablespoons sherry	30 ml
1½ teaspoons rice vinegar	7.5 ml
2 tablespoons sesame oil	30 ml
⅛ teaspoon stevioside	½ ml
or 1 teaspoon stevia blend	5 ml
or 2 packets of stevia	

Combine all ingredients together and use as a glaze over grilled meat.

Makes 8 servings

NUTRITIONAL FACTS PER SERVING: **14G CARBOHYDRATE;** 106 CALORIES; 4G TOTAL FAT; 1G PROTEIN • FOOD EXCHANGES: 1 FAT; 1 OTHER CARBOHYDRATES

Cranberry Sauce

A Thanksgiving favorite.

1 teaspoon stevioside	5 ml
or 8 teaspoons stevia blend	40 ml
or 16 packets of stevia	
1 cup white grape juice	235 ml
12 ounces fresh cranberries	345 g

In a saucepan, combine stevia and juice. Bring to a rapid boil. Add cranberries. Stirring constantly, boil gently over medium-high heat for 6-7 minutes or until cranberry skins pop. Remove from heat. Serve warm or chilled.

Makes about 3 cups (12 servings)

NUTRITIONAL FACTS PER SERVING: 7G CARBOHYDRATE; 27 CALORIES; TRACE TOTAL FAT; TRACE PROTEIN • FOOD EXCHANGES: ½ FRUIT

Blackberry Sauce (Jelly)

10 ounces blackberries	300 g
1 teaspoon lemon juice	5 ml
½ teaspoon vanilla	2.5 ml
¼ teaspoon stevioside	1.25 ml
or 2 teaspoons stevia blend	10 ml
or 4 packets of stevia	

In a food processor, process blackberries and lemon juice until smooth. Strain sauce to remove seeds. Mix in vanilla and stevia.

VARIATION:

To make a jelly, place sauce in a small saucepan and stir in 2 teaspoon of agar agar or 1 packet of gelatin. Slowly bring to a low boil, stirring constantly. Cook until thickened. Cool. Keeps in refrigerator for 4 weeks.

As a sauce, makes about 6 servings

NUTRITIONAL FACTS PER SERVING: 6G CARBOHYDRATE; 26 CALORIES; TRACE TOTAL FAT; TRACE PROTEIN • FOOD EXCHANGES: ½ FRUIT

Note: Sauce can be used as a topping on desserts such as ice cream, cheese cake or even crème brule. It can even be served on grilled chicken and is also wonderful over eggs. Experiment!

Gingered Pear Jam

12 ripe pears, diced	12 each
1 teaspoon stevioside	5 ml
or 8 teaspoons stevia blend	50 ml
or 16 packets of stevia	
3 pieces preserved ginger, diced	3 pieces
2 tablespoons lemon juice	30 ml
1 cup water, approximately	235 ml

Combine all ingredients in glass pan. Bring to a boil for 20 minutes or until mixture begins to gel. (You may need more water.) Pour into half-pint jars and process in boiling water bath for 10 minutes.

Makes 64 servings

NUTRITIONAL FACTS PER SERVING: 5G CARBOHYDRATE; 32 CALORIES; TRACE TOTAL FAT; TRACE PROTEIN • FOOD EXCHANGES: ½ FRUIT

Appendix

Sample Menus

The Average Day

DAY 1

Breakfast: *Carbohydrates*
Glass of milk. 12g
2 x cheese blintzes. 8g

Total carbohydrates. 20g

Lunch:
Protein Shake 2g

Dinner:
Caesar Salad 10g
Lasagna 8g
Berry Dreams 12g

Total carbohydrates. 30g

Daily total: 52g

DAY 2

Breakfast: *Carbohydrates*
4oz orange juice 12g
Pancakes topped with
   Kahlua Fudge sauce 15g

Total carbohydrates. 27g

Lunch:
Salad 10g
Grilled Chicken. 0g

Tota carbohydrates 10g

Dinner:
Curried Pumpkin Soup 6g
Pesto Roasted Cornish hen 0g
Steamed Cauliflower 5g
Slice of Protein Bread 3g
Lemon Granita 4g

Total carbohydrates. 18g

Daily total: 55g

DAY 3

Breakfast: *Carbohydrates*
Orange Dream 9g

Lunch:
Mock Potato Salad 3g
Roast beef Sandwich on protein
   bread 6g

Total carbohydrates. 9g

Dinner:
Suffed Jalapenos 2g
Lamb Curry 16g
Steamed Broccoli 10g
Vanilla Ice Cream 4g

Total carbohydrates. 32g

Daily Total: 50g

Special Occasions

THANKSGIVING   *Carbohydrates*

Cranberry Sauce 7g
Pumpkin Soup 6g
Salad 10g
Roasted Turkey 0g
Mock Potato Salad 3g
Pickled Eggs 0g
Wild Rice Stuffing. . . . .
Protein Bread 3g

Total carbohydrates . . . .   g

CHRISTMAS HOLIDAYS

Assorted meats and cheeses 10g
Stevia Deviled Eggs 0g
Baked Ham in Brown Aspic Sauce   0g
Romaine Salad 10g
Mushroom Soup 9g
Crème Brulee 5g
Egg Nog 9g

Total carbohydrates 38g

SPECIAL OCCASION PARTY SNACKS

Paprika Roasted Chicken Wings . . 2g
Stuffed Mushrooms with Cheese . 9g
Sesame Shrimp Cakes 7g
Shrimp Scampi 2g
Raspberry Tiramisu 4g
Dark Chocolate Candies 9g
Traditional Gelato 7g

Total carbohydrates 40g

Special Dinners

SOUTH OF THE BORDER   *Carbohydrates*

Avocado Soup 10g
Stuffed Jalapenos 2g
Cheese Tacos 10g
Jalapeno Ice Cream 9g

Total carbohydrates 31g

MIDDLE-EASTERN DELIGHT

Protein Crisps 5g
Eggplant Dip 6g
Crumbled Feta Cheese 2g
Black Olive Pate 4g
Tandoori Chicken 3g
Flan 8g

Total carbohydrates 28g

ORIENTAL NIGHTS

Egg Drop Soup 2g
Sesame Shrimp Cakes 7g
Chinese Pork Tenderloin 4g
Fried Strawberries 7g
Mango Mousse 11g

Total carbohydrates 31g

Stevia Conversions

For best results, use stevia extracts that contain at least 90% steviosides and read Chapters 5, Successful Cooking With Stevia.

Packets to Packets

Sugar	Stevia Blends (Spoonable Stevia)	Aspartame	Saccharin	Acesulfame-k	Sucralose (Splenda®)
1 packet	1 packet	1 packet	1 packet	1 packet	1 packet

Packets to packets stevia blends are equal in sweetening power to artificial sweeteners. However, stevia blends (spoonable stevia) in bulk are not necessarily equal to the spoonable or bulk forms of artificial sweeteners. Fortunately, most recipes call for packets of artificial sweeteners. Just convert the number of artificial sweetener packets to stevia blend (spoonable stevia), or if you prefer, use pure stevioside.

When replacing aspartame with stevia you must make some adjustments – stevia is heat stable, but aspartame will loose its sweetness when heated.

Artificial Sweetener Packets to Stevia Extracts

Artificial Sweetener (packets) or Sucralose (packets)	Stevia Blends (packets)	Stevia Blends (Spoonable Stevia) Bulk Form (teaspoons)	Clear Stevia Liquid (teaspoons)	Pure Stevioside (teaspoons)
1	1	½	about ¼	1/16
6	6	3	about ½	3/8
8	8	4	about ¾	½
12	12	6	1¼	¾
18	18	9	1⅓	1⅛
24	24	12	2½	1½
48	48	24	5¼	3

Avoid a Bitter Taste: Although stevia sweetening strengths vary form one brand to the next, when you use a brand high in steviosides, you can achieve a sweeter taste without bitterness. This chart is based on using an extract with over 90% steviosides. Consequently, when using a pure stevioside with less than 90% steviosides reduce the amount of stevioside listed in the chart above by 30% — the final product will not be as sweet, but you'll avoid a bitter taste.

Sugar, Sucralose (Splenda®) and Stevia Extracts

Sugar	Granulated Sucralose (Granulated Splenda®)	Stevia Blends (Spoonable Stevia) in Packets (packets)	Stevia Blends (Spoonable Stevia) Bulk Form (teaspoons)	Clear Stevia Liquid (teaspoons)	Pure Stevioside (teaspoons)
2 teaspoons	2 teaspoons	1	½	about ¼	1/16
¼ cup	¼ cup	6	3	about ½	3/8
⅓ cup	⅓ cup	8	4	about ¾	½
½ cup	½ cup	12	6	1¼	¾
¾ cup	¾ cup	18	9	1¾	1
1 cup	1 cup	24	12	2½	1½
2 cups	2 cups	48	24	5¼	3

Avoid a Bitter Taste: Although stevia sweetening strengths vary form one brand to the next, when you use a brand high in steviosides, you can achieve a sweeter taste without bitterness. This chart is based on using an extract with over 90% steviosides. Consequently, when using a pure stevioside with less than 90% steviosides reduce the amount of stevioside listed in the chart above by 30% — the final product will not be as sweet, but you'll avoid a bitter taste.

Glossary of Ingredients

Stevia can be difficult to cook with; it often has an herbal taste, does not caramelize like sugar and does not add volume like sugar. Therefore, special ingredients may be needed for the best results. Most special ingredients are available at health food stores, or on the Internet at www.SteviaSmart.com.

Agar—seaweed that is used for thickening. It is available at health food stores, or Asian grocery stores.

Ascorbic Acid—vitamin C. It is used to prevent browning of cut fruits and to help breads rise.

Cocoa Butter—the whitish yellow fat extracted from cocoa beans during the manufacture of chocolate. Cocoa Butter is often used in body care products - only purchase food grade Cocoa Butter for cooking.

Coconut oil—used in high heat cooking applications, as a substitute for shortening in baking or in natural body care. Always purchase a food grade oil for cooking.

Fearn Soya Powder®—a brand name of soy flour. The soybeans are cooked first then made into a powder. It has a nice smooth taste and is easier to digest than normal soy flour.

Gelatin—an odorless, colorless, tasteless thickening agent. It is used for both desserts and savory dishes. For a vegetarian alternative, use agar.

Ghee (clarified butter)—butter in which all of the nonfat elements have been removed. Excellent for cooking at high heat without burning.

Glycerin is a natural or synthetic emollient. Generally used in soap and cosmetic applications, it has a mild sweet taste with a low glycemic level. Glycerin adds taste and texture to sugar-free baked goods.

Isolated soy protein—the extracted protein from the soybean. This is often referred to as "soy protein powder" and is normally used to make protein shakes. The first ingredient should be "isolated soy protein" with no added sweeteners.

Isolated whey protein and whey protein concentrate—can be used inter-changeably—This is often referred to as "whey protein powder" and is normally used to make protein shakes. The first ingredient in whey protein powder should be "isolated whey protein" or "whey protein concentrate" and it should be unsweetened.

Liquid Lecithin—a vitamin that is normally derived from soybeans adds texture and binding to baked goods.

Milk & Egg Protein Powder (MLO Products®)—contains whey protein concentrate, calcium sodium caseinate, and egg albumen. These ingredients help give home made protein bars its great taste and texture. Any brand of this combination should do. If it is unavailable you may substitute pure whey protein.

Nut Flour—finely ground nuts to form a fine powder.

Nut meal—nuts which are ground to form a corse powder.

Paraffin Wax—fully refined, food grade wax is used in candy making.

Rolled Oat Flour—also called "oat flour." Available pre-made, or place rolled oats in a blender or food processor and puree until the desired texture.

Soya Powder®—see Fearn Soya Powder®

Stevia—natural sweetener available at health food stores. There are many different types of stevia. For best results use the highest quality available.

Stevia Blends—due to the great strength of pure stevioside, many manufac-turers have added a flowing agent like maltodextrin, FOS, or erythritol. This makes the stevia easier to measure. Although sweetness varies from brand to brand, most Stevia Blends are 4 to 5 times sweeter than sugar.

Stevia Liquid (Dark Green)—syrup made of the whole leaves of the plant, Stevia Rebuadiani Bertoni.

Stevia Liquid (Other)—this refers to liquids in which pure Steviosides and Rebaudiosides have been suspended in water.

Stevioside (Steviosides)—refers to the sweet molecules found in the plant Stevia Rebuadiani Bertoni. This plant also contains the sweet molecules, Rebaudiosides. The combined extraction of steviosides and rebaudiosides makes a "pure stevia extract" about 300 times sweeter than sugar. (This extract is referred to as "stevioside" throughout this book). The higher percentage of steviosides and rebaudiosides the better tasting the product.

Super Strength Flavoring (LorAnn® Gourmet Flavorings)—extracts used in professional baking and cooking. A few drops, not teaspoons, are used to add great flavor.

Tragacanth Gum—natural powder used as an emulsifier and thickener. Also used in cake decorating to make gum paste.

Vital Wheat Gluten (gluten flour, instant gluten flour, pure gluten flour)—wheat flour with the starch and bran removed. This natural wheat protein binds moisture and traps air, making breads rise better and baked goods moister. Perfect for low-carbohydrate baking and cooking

Xanthan Gum—gives volume to breads. Can be added to liquids such as gravies, sauces, and salad dressing to give a thick creamy smooth texture. A good stabilizer.

Suppliers of Stevia Extracts and Plants

The following is a list of most major stevia manufactures that offer a variety of stevia products. Their stevia products are available in health food stores or direct from the manufacture. This list is for informational purposes only to help you, the consumer, locate stevia supplements. Visit www.cookingwithstevia.com for a more complete list and updates.

NOW Foods
395 S. Glen Ellen Rd.
Bloomingdale, IL 60108
www.nowvitamins.com
800-999-8069

NuNaturals
2220 W. 2nd Ave. #1
Eugene, OR 97402
www.nunaturals.com
800-753-4372

Stevia Smart
P.O. Box 171683
Arlington, TX 76003
www.SteviaSmart.com
888-798-7999

Stevita Co., Inc.
(Certified Organic Stevia)
7650 US Hwy. 287, #100
Arlington, Texas 76001
www.stevitastevia.com
888-STEVITA
888 783-8482

Wisdom of the Ancients
2546 W. Birchwood Ave., Suite 104
Mesa, AZ 85202
www.wisdomherbs.com
800-899-9908
www.wisdomherbs.com

The Herbal Advantage
www.herbaladvantage.com
131 Bobwhite Rd.
Rogersville, MO 65742
800-753-9199

Mountain Valley Growers
www.mountainvalleygrowers.com
Sellers of Certified Organic Stevia Plants (Scientific Certification Systems).
38325 Pepperweed Rd.
Squaw Valley, CA 93675
559-338-2775

Stevia Petition

Stevia is a sweetener that is currently being discriminated against by the FDA. Contact your Representative today and let them know that you want to use Stevia! Fight the injustice of the FDA!

Stevia is a natural sweetener used internationally by millions - except in the United States. This herb is being discriminated against by the Food and Drug Administration (FDA). You can fight this injustice by contacting your government representatives today!

Photocopy this petition, fill it out and mail it to your Congressional Representative and your two Senate Representatives. With your help, we will win this battle.

This petition is also available on-line at www.CookingWithStevia.org.

NAME

ADDRESS

CITY, STATE, ZIP

COUNTRY

HOME PHONE

E-MAIL ADDRESS

DATE

REPRESENTATIVE'S NAME

ADDRESS

Dear _____:

I am writing to express my outrage at the Food and Drug Administration's mishandling of the herb STEVIA in the United States. While other nations are able to use this wonderful herb as a sugar substitute, Americans are limited to using it as a "dietary supplement". Why is this? STEVIA is approved for use as a food and food ingredient in countries around the world because it is all-natural, non-toxic, non-caloric, helpful to the environment, a valuable cash crop and safe for diabetics, hence completely safe for human use, but FDA restricts its use by Americans. Effectively banned within the United States, STEVIA plants are rarely even grown by American farmers.

With the passage of the 1994 Dietary Supplement Health and Education Act (DSHEA), Congress rightly gave the power back to the people concerning whether or not to improve their health with the use of natural products previously kept out of reach. DSHEA also permitted Americans to use STEVIA but only as a dietary supplement. Despite this legal protection, the FDA has done everything within it's power to try to prevent the importation and distribution of STEVIA in the United States. Petitions to have STEVIA receive GRAS (Generally Accepted as Safe) status were denied by the FDA. FDA employs delay tactics, such as requesting unreasonable amounts of statistical data about this plant's agricultural and commercial history prior to 1958.

In 1997, the CBS news magazine 60 Minutes aired a report revealing a conflict of interest between FDA and one manufacturer of artificial sweeteners. This manufacturer had "influenced" the director of the FDA to get the approval of aspartame as a food additive during the 1980s when there were many questionable reports on its safety. Today the FDA receives more complaints about aspartame than about any other product. It is believed that the cozy relationship between FDA and the artificial sweetener industry is why STEVIA has largely been kept out of reach of the American consumer.

Is STEVIA safe? Absolutely. Research proves this—research the FDA ignores. Moreover, STEVIA has been used extensively around the world as an ingredient in foods WITHOUT A SINGLE CASE OF UNDESIRABLE EFFECTS. This fact alone should qualify as proof that the product is safe for use as an all-natural sweetener.

Do the American people want STEVIA? Count on it. Americans are more and more averse to the use of artificial substances in their diets. The herb STEVIA is especially beneficial for people who suffer from diabetes, hypoglycemia, candida and other ailments where regular use of sugar and artificial sweeteners is ill-advised.

As my elected representative, I am requesting that you review the entire controversy surrounding the herb STEVIA. FDA's unconscionable withholding of this natural substance from the American people must be answered, once and for all.

Make good on DSHEA. Give STEVIA full legal status.

Yours truly,

References

Alverez, Mauro, "Contraceptive effect of the Stevia and of its sweetening principles", State University of Maringa, Dept. of Pharmacy and Pharmacology, Maringa, Brazil, October 1994.

Bonvie, Linda and Bill, and Gates, Donna, "The Stevia Story. A tale of incredible sweetness and intrigue" B.E.D. Publications, Atlanta, GA. p. 13–71.

Crammer, B., and R. Ikan. "Progress in the chemistry and properties of rebaudioside." Greenby, T.H., editor. Developments in Sweeteners. London, Elsevier, vol 3:45-64, 1987.

Ishii, Emy L.; Schwab, Andreas J.; Bracht, Adelar, "Inhibition of monosaccharide transport in the intact rat liver by stevioside". Departamento de Farmacia-Bioquimica, Universidade de Maringa; and Institut for Physiologische Chemie, Physikalische Biochemie und Zellbiologie der Universität München. Printed in Biochemical Pharmacology, Vol. 36, No. 9, pp. 1417-1433, 1987.

Kerr, Warwick E., Mello, Maria Luiza S., and Bonadio, Evangelina, "Mutagenicity tests on the stevioside from Stevia rebaudiana (BERT.) Bertoni"

Kinghorn, A. Douglas, "Food Ingredient Safety Review: Stevia rebaudiana leaves", (March 16, 1992).

Kinghorn, A. D.; Soejarto, D. D.; Katz, N. L.; Kamath, S. K. "Studies to identify, idsolate, develop and test naturally occurring noncariogenic sweeteners that my be used as dietary sucrose substitutes." (Univ. Illinois, Chicago, Il. USA). Report 1983

Kleber, Carl J., "Rat dental caries investigation of stevioside natural sweetener", Purdue University, April 24, 1990.

Klongpanichpak, S., P. Temcharoen, C. Toskulkao, S. Apibal, and T. Glinsukon. "Lack of mutagenicity of stevioside and steviol in Salmonella typhimurium TA 98 and TA 100." Journal Medical Associations of Thailand, Sep; 80, Suppl 1:S121-128, 1997.

Matsui M., K. Matsui, Y. Kawasaki, Y. Oda, T. Noguchi, "Evaluation of the genotoxicity of stevioside and steviol using six in vitro and one in vivo mutagenicity assays." Mutagenesis, 11:573-579, 1996.

Nakayama, Kunio; Kasahara, Daigo; Yamamoto, Fumihiro, "Absorption, distribution, metabolism and excretion of Stevioside in Rats". Omiya Research

Laboratory, Nikken Chemicals Co. Ltd.: 1-346, Kitabukuro-cho, Omiya, Saitama, Japan. March 1985

Nunes, P., and N.A. Pereira. "The effects of stevia rebaudiana on the fertility of experimental animals." Revista Brasileira de Farmacia, 69:46-50, 1988.

Pinheiro, Carlos Eduardo, "Effect of the Stevioside and of the aqueous extract of Stevia Rebaudiana (BERT) Bertoni on the glycemia of normal and diabetic rats", Presented to the II Brazilian Convention on Stevia rebaudiana (Bert) Bertoni, September 1982

Richard, David, "Stevia Rebaudiana, Nature's sweet secret". Vital Health Publishins, Bloomingdale, IL. p. 732.

Smoliar VI, Karpilovskaia ED, Salii NS, Tsapko EV, Lavrushenko LF, Gulich MP, Kryshevich LP, Grigorenko SN. [Effect of a new sweetening agent from Stevia rebaudiana on animals]. Vopr Pitan 1992 Jan-Feb;(1):60-3 [Article in Russian] PMID: 1621383, UI: 92320722

"Stevia Rebaudiana: Description and Chemical Aspects", Inga S.A., Maringa, Brazil, 1989

Uehara, Olivia A.; Utino, Vivian H.; Miyata, Ivete; and Oliveira, Ricardo M. Filho, "Interaction of the stevioside with androgens" as presented to the 2nd Brazilian seminar on Stevia rebaudiana (BERT.) Bertoni. Dept. of Pharmacology, Institute of Medical Sciences, University of Sao Paulo.

Zhou, Ren; Ran, Zhijun; Li, Qiang; Zi, Xueli; Rong, Yingxin; Li, Renbiao, "Ion exchange methods in extraction and purification of steviosides from Stevia rebaudiana." Dep. Chem., Yunnan Norinal Univ., Peoples Republic of China. 1984

Internet References:

Aspartame Consumer Safety network
web2.airmail.net/marystod

Herb Reasearch Foundation
www.herbs.org

Journalists Linda and Bill Bonvie
members.bellatlantic.net/~boncom/

Cooking With Stevia
www.CookingWithStevia.com

Low-Carbohydrate References

Paleolithic Diet
http://www.beyondveg.com/cat/paleodiet/index.shtml

Stone-Age Diet
http://www.nutritionreporter.com/stone_age_diet.html

USDA Nutrient Database
http://www.nal.usda.gov/fnic/cgi-bin/nut_search.pl

Information on glycogen
www.usatf.org/wwwboard/messages/1712.html

Glycemic Index of Foods
http://www.diabetesnet.com/gi.html

Information on sugar consumption
http://buglady.clc.uc.edu/biology/bio111/pop.htm

A. George F. Davidson, BSc, MD, Eric G. Hassall, MD. "Screening for Celiac Disease." Can Med Assoc. J., Sept 1, 1997; 157:547-8

Baba NH, Sawaya S, Torbay N, Habbal Z, Azar S, Hashim SA. [High protein vs high carbohydrate hypoenergetic diet for the treatment of obese hyperinsulinemic subjects]. Int J Obes Relat Metab Disord 1999 Nov;23(11):1202-6

Davidson, A. George F., BSc, MD; Eric G. Hassall, MD. "Screening for celiac disease." Canadian Medical Association Journal, Sept 1, 1997; 157 (5).

Klongpanichpak S, Temcharoen P, Toskulkao C, Apibal S, Glinsukon T. [Lack of mutagenicity of stevioside and steviol in Salmonella typhimurium TA 98 and TA 100.] J Med Assoc Thai 1997 Sep;80 Suppl 1:S121-8. Department of Physiology, Faculty of Science, Mahidol University, Bangkok, Thailand. PMID: 9347659, UI: 98007251

Ste. Marie, Micheline T., MD. "Celiac Disease: Something to Worry About?". Nova Scotia Celiac News, August–October, 1998.

Skov AR, Toubro S, Bulow J, Krabbe K, Parving HH, Astrup A. [Changes in renal function during weight loss induced by high vs low-protein low-fat diets in overweight subjects]. Int J Obes Relat Metab Disord 1999 Nov;23(11):1170-7

Trier, Jerry S., "Celiac Sprue". New England Journal of Medicine, Dec. 12, 1991, Vol. 325 No. 24, pp 1709-1716.

Index

Visit the web site of Cooking With Stevia for upcoming book information, the latest news, and recipes for stevia, the naturally sweet herb.

http://www.CookingWithStevia.com

About the Author

James Kirkland, B.B.A., is a well-known stevia expert and health industry consultant. Mr. Kirkland's years of stevia research and experience as a chef and caterer give him keen insight on cooking with nature's no-calorie sweetener. In addition to writing books and articles, Mr. Kirkland teaches sugar-free cooking classes and gives radio and television interviews. He is also a co-founder of Stevia Activists, a grass roots group seeking to educate the general public about the many benefits of the naturally sweet, safe, and calorie-free stevia herb. Mr. Kirkland also co-authored *Sugar-Free Cooking With Stevia*.

Sugar-Free Cooking With STEVIA:
The Naturally Sweet and Calorie-Free Herb

by James and Tanya Kirkland

ISBN 1-928906-15-X

Stevia is a unique herb that has been used internationally for centuries as a non-caloric sweetener. It is safe for diabetics and can prevent cavities. The FDA actually banned this remarkable and informative cookbook in an attempt to suppress information about Stevia's amazing sweetening abilities and excellent safety record. Read more about the controversy in Chapter 3, 'Stevia, the FDA and the First Amendment'. Sugar-Free Cooking With Stevia contains over 200 family favorites. With more than 40 pages of informative text and easy-to-follow stevia conversion charts, this book makes it easy for anyone to enjoy delicious, healthy sugar-free foods.